easy to make!
Meat-free Meals

Good Housekeeping

easy to make!
Meat-free
Meals

COLLINS & BROWN

This edition published in Great Britain in 2011
by Collins & Brown
10 Southcombe Street
London W14 0RA

An imprint of Anova Books Company Ltd.

First publshed in Great Britain in 2009

The Good Housekeeping website is
www.allaboutyou.com/goodhousekeeping

10 9 8 7 6 5 4 3 2

ISBN 978-1-84340-644-0

A catalogue record for this book is available from the British
Library.

Reproduction by Dot Gradations Ltd
Printed and bound by Times Offset (M) Sdn. Bhd, Malaysia

This book can be ordered direct from the publisher at
www.anovabooks.com

NOTES

- Both metric and imperial measures are given for the recipes. Follow either set of measures, not a mixture of both, as they are not interchangeable.
- All spoon measures are level.
  1 tsp = 5ml spoon; 1 tbsp = 15ml spoon.
- Ovens and grills must be preheated to the specified temperature.
- Use sea salt and freshly ground black pepper unless otherwise suggested.
- Fresh herbs should be used unless dried herbs are specified in a recipe.
- Medium eggs should be used except where otherwise specified. Free-range eggs are recommended.
- Note that certain recipes, including mayonnaise, lemon curd and some cold desserts, contain raw or lightly cooked eggs. The young, elderly, pregnant women and anyone with an immune-deficiency disease should avoid these, because of the slight risk of salmonella.
- Calorie, fat and carbohydrate counts per serving are provided for the recipes.
- If you are following a gluten- or dairy-free diet, check the labels on all pre-packaged food goods.
- Recipe serving suggestions do not take gluten- or dairy-free diets into account.

Picture Credits
Photographers: Martin Brigdale (pages 75, 82, 92); Nicki Dowey
(pages 33, 36, 38, 39, 40, 44, 47, 48, 52, 54, 55, 57, 58, 59, 61,
62, 64, 65, 66, 67, 68, 73, 74, 77, 80, 85, 90, 91, 94, 96, 99, 100,
103, 105, 106, 111, 113, 114, 117, 118, 120, 121, 125, 126); Will
Heap (pages 76, 101); Craig Robertson (Basics photography plus
pages 34, 35, 37, 45, 60, 78, 81, 97, 112, 115, 119, 122, 124);
Lucinda Symons (pages 28, 43, 46, 53, 84, 88, 93, 98, 104).

Contents

Foreword

Cooking, for me, is one of life's great pleasures. Not only is it necessary to fuel your body, but it exercises creativity, skill, social bonding and patience. The science behind the cooking also fascinates me, learning to understand how yeast works, or to grasp why certain flavours marry quite so well (in my mind) is to become a good cook.

I've often encountered people who claim not to be able to cook – they're just not interested or say they simply don't have time. My sister won't mind me saying that she was one of those who sat firmly in the camp of disinterested domestic goddess. But things change, she realised that my mother (an excellent cook) can't always be on hand to prepare steaming home-cooked meals and that she actually wanted to become a mother one day who was able to whip up good food for her own family. All it took was some good cook books (naturally, Good Housekeeping was present and accounted for) and some enthusiasm and sure enough she is now a kitchen wizard, creating such confections that even baffle me.

I've been lucky enough to have had a love for all things culinary since as long as I can remember. Baking rock-like chocolate cakes and misshapen biscuits was a right of passage that I protectively guard. I made my mistakes young, so have lost the fear of cookery mishaps. I think it's these mishaps that scare people, but when you realise that a mistake made once will seldom be repeated, then kitchen domination can start.

This Good Housekeeping Easy to Make! collection is filled with hundreds of tantalising recipes that have been triple tested (at least!) in our dedicated test kitchens. They have been developed to be easily achievable, delicious and guaranteed to work – taking the chance out of cooking.

I hope you enjoy this collection and that it inspires you to get cooking.

Meike.

Meike Beck
Cookery Editor
Good Housekeeping

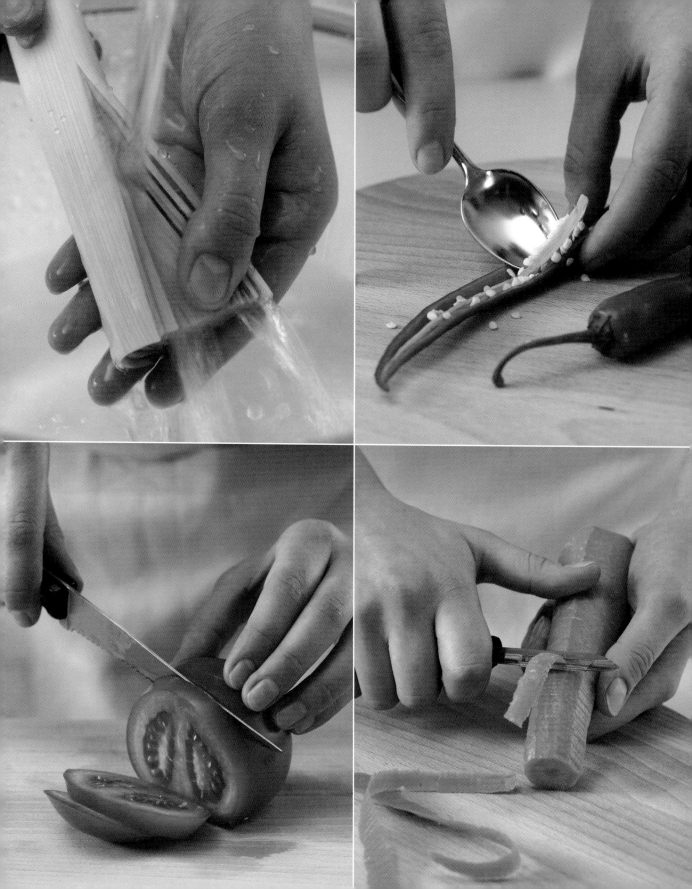

0

The Basics

Vegetarian and vegan diets

The huge variety of fresh vegetables, fruits, nuts, seeds, spices and herbs makes it easy to cook a wide range of tasty, nutritious vegetarian meals. To make shopping easier, many products suitable for vegetarians are now clearly labelled and easy to identify – including invaluable ingredients such as vegetarian cheeses and stocks. Some vegetarians might not want to eat gelatine, animal fats such as lard and suet, and animal rennet in non-vegetarian cheeses. However, the majority eat dairy produce, including milk, vegetarian cheeses and free -range eggs. Vegans follow a more restricted diet, which also excludes all dairy products, eggs, and even foods like honey.

Importance of a balanced diet

As with any diet, variety is all important. Provided a vegetarian diet includes a good range of cereals and grains, pulses, nuts and seeds, fruit and vegetables, dairy and/or soya products, it should be nutritionally sound. A small quantity of plant oils, margarine or butter is needed to provide essential fatty acids and vitamins.

Meat-free living

Cooking vegetarian food is a great chance to be creative and inventive. There are so many spices, herbs, pulses and grains waiting to be combined with pasta and luscious fresh vegetables.

Nutrient	**Sourced from**
Protein	**Nuts:** Hazelnuts, brazils, almonds, cashews, walnuts, pinenuts, macadamias, pecan, peanuts and peanut butter
	Seeds: Sesame, pumpkin, sunflower, linseeds
	Grains/cereals: Wheat (in bread and flour, pasta, etc.), barley, rye, oats, millet, maize (sweetcorn), rice
	Soya products: Tofu, tempeh*, textured vegetable protein, veggie burgers, soya milk (*tempeh is made from soya beans and is a staple protein in Indonesian cooking. It's similar to tofu but has a richer flavour and firmer texture)
	Dairy products: Milk, cheese, yogurt (butter and cream are very poor sources of protein)
	Eggs
	Pulses: Beans, chickpeas and lentils
Carbohydrate	Fruit
	Milk
	Sugar
	Cereals and grains: Bread, rice, pasta, oats, barley, millet, buckwheat, rye
	Root vegetables: Potatoes, parsnips
Vitamins	**Vitamin A:** Red, orange or yellow vegetables such as carrots, sweet potatoes, peppers and tomatoes; leafy green vegetables such as spinach and watercress; fruits such as apricots, peaches, papayas, orange-fleshed melons
	Vitamin B: Yeasts, whole cereals (especially wheat germ), nuts and seeds, pulses, green vegetables
	Vitamin B12: Eggs, yeast extracts, soya milks, veggie burgers
	Vitamin C: Fruit, potatoes, salad, vegetables especially leafy green vegetables
	Vitamin E: Vegetable oil, wholegrain cereals, eggs, avocados, nuts
	Vitamin K: Vegetables, cereals

Sources of protein

Most vegetarians needn't worry about getting enough protein: this nutrient is found in a wide variety of foods, including pulses, tofu and other soya bean products, Quorn, eggs, cheese, sprouted beans and seeds.

Meat substitutes

Pulses

The term pulse is used to describe all of the various beans, peas and lentils. They are highly nutritious, especially when eaten with grains, such as couscous, pasta, rice or bread. Dried pulses should be stored in airtight containers in a cool, dry cupboard. They keep well, but after about six months their skins start to toughen and they take progressively longer to cook the longer they are stored. Canned pulses are a convenient, quick alternative to soaking and cooking dried ones and most supermarkets stock a wide range. A 400g can (drained weight about 235g) is roughly equivalent to 100g (3½oz) dried beans. The dried beans double in weight after soaking.

Sprouted beans and seeds

These are rich in nutrients and lend a nutty taste and crunchy texture to salads and stir-fries. Fresh bean sprouts are available from most supermarkets. Many beans and seeds can be sprouted at home, though it is important to buy ones that are specifically produced for sprouting – from a healthfood shop or other reliable source. Mung beans, aduki beans, alfalfa seeds and fenugreek are all suitable.

Vegetarian cheeses

Some vegetarians prefer to avoid cheeses that have been produced by the traditional method, because this uses animal-derived rennet. Most supermarkets and cheese shops now stock an excellent range of vegetarian cheeses, produced using vegetarian rennet, which comes from plants, such as thistle and mallow, that contain enzymes capable of curdling milk.

Tofu

Also known as bean curd, tofu is made from ground soya beans in a process akin to cheese-making. It is highly nutritious but virtually tasteless. However, it readily absorbs other flavours when marinaded.

Tofu is sold as a chilled product and should be stored in the fridge. Once the packet is opened, the tofu should be kept immersed in a bowl of water in the fridge and eaten within four days.

Firm tofu is usually cut into chunks, then immersed in tasty marinades or dressings prior to grilling, stir-frying, deep-frying, adding to stews, or tossing raw into salads. It can also be chopped and made into burgers and nut roasts.

Smoked tofu has more flavour than unsmoked; it is used in the same way but doesn't need marinating.

Silken tofu is softer and creamier than firm tofu and is useful for making sauces and dressings.

Textured Vegetable Protein (TVP)

This forms the bulk of most ready-prepared vegetarian burgers, sausages and mince. It is made from a mixture of soya flour, flavourings and liquid, which is cooked, then extruded under pressure and cut into chunks or small pieces to resemble mince. It has a slightly chewy, meat-like texture. TVP can be included in stews, pies, curries and other dishes, rather as meat would be used by non-vegetarians.

Quorn

Quorn is a vegetarian product derived from a distant relative of the mushroom. Although it is not suitable for vegans because it contains egg albumen, Quorn is a good source of complete protein for vegetarians. Like tofu, Quorn has a bland flavour and benefits from being marinated before cooking. Available from the chiller cabinet, quorn should be kept in the fridge.

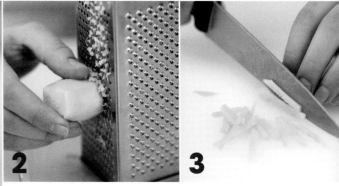

Ginger

1 **Grating** Cut off a piece of the root and peel with a vegetable peeler. Cut off any brown spots.

2 Rest the grater on a board or small plate and grate the ginger. Discard any large fibres adhering to the pulp.

3 **Slicing, shredding and chopping** Cut slices off the ginger and cut off the skin carefully. Cut off any brown spots. Stack the slices and cut into shreds. To chop, stack the shreds and cut across into small pieces.

4 **Pressing** If you just need the ginger juice, peel and cut off any brown spots, then cut into small chunks and use a garlic press held over a small bowl to extract the juice.

Flavourings

Garlic is one of the most widely used flavourings around the world. Asian dishes often use garlic, ginger and spring onions as the basic flavourings. Spicier dishes may include chillies, lemongrass or a prepared spice paste such as Thai curry paste.

Spring onions

Cut off the roots and trim any coarse or withered green parts. Slice diagonally, or shred by cutting into 5cm (2in) lengths and then slicing down the lengths, or chop finely, according to the recipe.

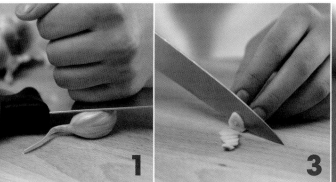

Garlic

1 Put the clove on a chopping board and place the flat side of a large knife on top of it. Press down firmly on the flat of the blade to crush the clove and break the papery skin.

2 Cut off the base of the clove and slip the garlic out of its skin. It should come away easily.

3 **Slicing** Using a rocking motion with the knife tip on the board, slice the garlic as thinly as you need.

4 **Shredding and chopping** Holding the slices together, shred them across the slices. Chop the shreds if you need chopped garlic.

5 **Crushing** After step 2, the whole clove can be put into a garlic press. To crush with a knife: roughly chop the peeled cloves with a pinch of salt. Press down hard with the edge of a large knife tip (with the blade facing away from you), then drag the blade along the garlic while still pressing hard. Continue to do this, dragging the knife tip over the garlic.

Chillies

1 Cut off the cap and slit open lengthways. Using a spoon, scrape out the seeds and the pith.

2 For diced chilli, cut into thin shreds lengthways, then cut crossways.

Cook's Tip

Wash hands thoroughly after handling chillies – the volatile oils will sting if accidentally rubbed into your eyes.

Mushrooms

Button, white, chestnut and flat mushrooms are all prepared in a similar way.

1 Wipe with a damp cloth or pastry brush to remove any dirt.

2 With button mushrooms, cut off the stalk flush with the base of the cap. For other mushrooms, cut a thin disc off the end of the stalk and discard. Chop or slice the mushrooms.

Preparing vegetables

These frequently used vegetables can be quickly prepared to add flavour to savoury dishes: onions and shallots have a pungent taste that becomes milder when they are cooked, while tomatoes and peppers add depth and richness to a variety of dishes.

Cook's Tips
- -

To roast asparagus, drizzle with olive oil, a few spoonfuls of water and a little salt and roast in a preheated oven, 200°C (180°C fan oven) mark 6, for 12–15 minutes, depending on the thickness of the asparagus.

To cook in water, heat a large pan of salted water that will hold the asparagus in a single layer. Put in the spears and simmer for 5 minutes until tender, then drain.

Asparagus

1 Cut or snap off the woody stem of each asparagus spear about 5cm (2in) from the stalk end, or where the white and green sections meet. Or cut off the stalk end and peel with a vegetable peeler or small sharp knife.

Fennel

1 Trim off the top stems and the base of the bulbs. Remove the core with a small sharp knife if it seems tough.

2 The outer leaves may be discoloured and can be scrubbed gently in cold water, or you can peel away the discoloured parts with a knife or a vegetable peeler. Slice the fennel or cut it into quarters, according to your recipe.

Leeks

As some leeks harbour a lot of grit and earth between their leaves, they need careful cleaning.

1 Cut off the root and any tough parts of the leek. Make a cut into the leaf end of the leek, about 7.5cm (3in) deep.

2 Hold under the cold tap while separating the cut halves to expose any grit. Wash well, then shake dry. Use the green tops for stock.

Seeding tomatoes

1 Halve the tomato through the core. Use a spoon or a small sharp knife to remove the seeds and juice. Shake off the excess liquid.

2 Chop the tomato as required for your recipe and place in a colander for a minute or two, to drain off any excess liquid.

Peeling tomatoes

1 Fill a bowl or pan with boiling water. Using a slotted spoon, carefully add the tomato and leave for 15–30 seconds, then remove to a chopping board.

2 Use a small sharp knife to cut out the core in a single cone-shaped piece. Discard the core.

3 Peel off the skin; it should come away easily, depending on ripeness.

Cutting tomatoes

1 Use a small sharp knife to cut out the core in a single cone-shaped piece. Discard the core.

2 **Wedges** Halve the tomato and then cut into quarters or into three.

3 **Slices** Hold the tomato with the cored side on the chopping board for greater stability and use a serrated knife to cut into slices.

Classic Tomato Sauce

To serve 4, you will need:
1 tbsp olive oil, 1 small onion, chopped, 1 carrot, grated, 1 celery stick, chopped, 1 garlic clove, crushed, ½ tbsp tomato purée, 2 x 400g cans plum tomatoes, 1 bay leaf, ½ tsp oregano, 2 tsp caster sugar.

1 Heat the oil in a pan. Add the onion, carrot and celery, then fry gently for 20 minutes until softened.

2 Add the garlic and tomato purée and fry for 1 minute. Stir in the tomatoes, add the bay leaf, oregano and sugar and simmer for 30 minutes until thickened.

Avocados

Prepare avocados just before serving because their flesh discolours quickly once exposed to air.

 Halve the avocado lengthways and twist the two halves apart. Tap the stone with a sharp knife, then twist to remove the stone.

 Run a knife between the flesh and skin and pull away. Slice the flesh.

Seeding peppers

The seeds and white pith of peppers taste bitter so should be removed.

1 Cut off the top of the pepper, then cut away and discard the seeds and white pith.

2 Alternatively, cut the pepper in half vertically and snap out the white pithy core and seeds. Trim away the rest of the white membrane with a knife.

Chargrilling peppers

Charring imparts a smoky flavour and makes peppers easier to peel.

1 Hold the pepper, using tongs, over the gas flame on your hob (or under a preheated grill) until the skin blackens, turning until black all over.

2 Put in a bowl, cover and leave to cool (the steam will help to loosen the skin). Peel.

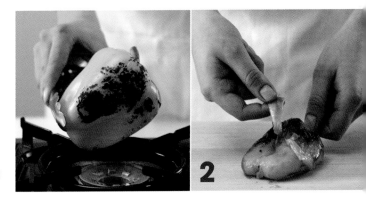

Spicy Red Pepper Dip

To serve 8, you will need:
3 large red peppers, about 450g (1lb) total weight, halved, 200g tub reduced-fat soft cheese, ½ tsp hot pepper sauce.

1 Preheat the grill. Chargrill the peppers as above, then peel and seed.

2 Put the flesh in a food processor or blender with the remaining ingredients. Purée until smooth. Cover and leave to chill for at least 2 hours to let the flavours develop. Taste and adjust the seasoning if necessary.

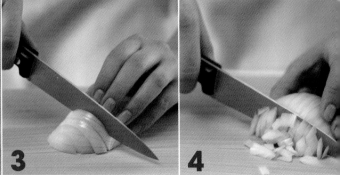

Onions

1 Cut off the tip and base of the onion. Peel away all the layers of papery skin and any discoloured layers underneath.

2 Put the onion root end down on the chopping board, then, using a sharp knife, cut the onion in half from tip to base.

3 **Slicing** Put one half on the board with the cut surface facing down and slice across the onion.

4 **Chopping** Slice the halved onions from the root end to the top at regular intervals. Next, make 2–3 horizontal slices through the onion, then slice vertically across the width.

Shallots

1 Cut off the tip and trim off the ends of the root. Peel off the skin and any discoloured layers underneath.

2 Holding the shallot with the root end down, use a small sharp knife to make deep parallel slices almost down to the base while keeping the slices attached to it.

3 **Slicing** Turn the shallot on its side and cut off slices from the base.

4 **Dicing** Make deep parallel slices at right angles to the first slices. Turn the shallot on its side and cut off the slices from the base. You should now have fine dice, but chop any larger pieces individually.

Carrots

1 Using a sharp knife, trim off the ends.

2 Using a vegetable peeler, peel off the skin in long strips.

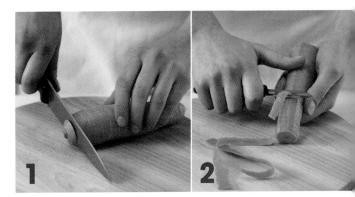

Cutting aubergines

1 Trim the aubergine to remove the stalk and end.

2 **Slicing** Cut the aubergine into slices as thick as the pieces you will need for your recipe.

3 **Cutting and dicing** Stack the slices and cut across them to the appropriate size for fingers. Cut in the opposite direction for dice.

Stuffing aubergines

1 To hollow out an aubergine for stuffing, cut off the stalk and halve the aubergine lengthways.

2 Make deep incisions in the flesh, using a crisscross pattern, being careful not to pierce the skin.

3 Using a spoon, scoop out the flesh, leaving the skin intact, and use according to your recipe.

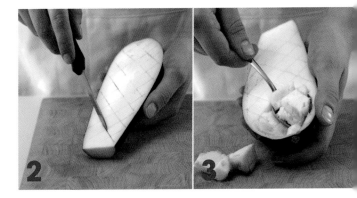

Using beans and lentils

Many dried beans and peas need to be soaked overnight before cooking. Lentils do not need soaking and are quicker to cook. Quicker still are canned beans: they are ready to use, but should be drained in a sieve and rinsed in cold water first.

Cooking beans

1 Pick through the beans to remove any grit or small stones. Put the beans in a bowl or pan and pour cold water over them to cover generously. Leave to soak for at least 8 hours, then drain. (If you are in a hurry, pour boiling water over and leave the beans to cool in the water for 1–2 hours.)

2 Put the soaked beans in a large pan and add cold water to cover by at least 5cm (2in). Bring to the boil and boil rapidly for 10 minutes.

3 Skim off the scum that rises to the top, turn down the heat and leave to simmer until the beans are soft inside. They should be tender but not falling apart. Check periodically to make sure there's enough water to keep the beans well covered. Drain well. If using in a salad, allow to cool completely.

Cooking times

Times vary for different dried beans, lentils and peas. Older beans take longer to cook, so check the 'best before' date. For some pulses, such as red kidney beans, aduki beans, black-eyed beans, black beans and borlotti beans, it is essential to cover them with fresh cold water, bring to the boil and boil rapidly for 10 minutes to destroy any toxins present in their skins. Then reduce the heat and cook at a steady simmer for the following times:

Chickpeas	1–2 hours
Red kidney, cannellini, borlotti, butter, flageolet beans	1–3 hours
Red lentils	20 minutes
Green lentils	30–40 minutes

Preparing long-grain rice

Long-grain rice needs no special preparation, though basmati should be washed to remove excess starch.

1 Put in a bowl and cover with cold water. Stir until this becomes cloudy, then drain and repeat the washing process until the water is clear.

2 Soak the rice for 30 minutes, then drain before cooking.

Cooking rice, grains and pasta

There are two main types of rice: long-grain and short-grain. Short-grain rice is used for dishes such as risotto, sushi and paella. Long-grain rice is generally used as an accompaniment or in salads. With any grain, the cooking time depends on how the grain has been processed. Cooked couscous, bulgur wheat and quinoa are all great in salads, as is pasta.

Cooking long-grain rice

1 Measure the rice by volume and put it in a pan with a pinch of salt with twice the volume of boiling water (or boiling stock).

2 Bring to the boil. Turn the heat down to low, and set the timer for the time stated on the pack. It needs to cook al dente: tender but with a hint of bite at the centre.

3 When the rice is cooked, fluff up the grains by gently tossing with a fork; this keeps the grains from sticking together. For using in salads, toss with a little salad dressing of your choice and leave to cool.

Perfect rice

- Use 50–75g (2–3oz) raw rice per person – or measure by volume 50–75ml (2–2½fl oz).
- If you often cook rice, you may want to invest in a special rice steamer. They are available in Asian supermarkets and some kitchen shops and give good, consistent results.

Couscous

Often mistaken for a grain, couscous is actually a type of pasta that originated in North Africa. It is perfect for making into salads or serving with stews and casseroles. The tiny pellets do not require cooking and can simply be soaked.

1 Measure the couscous in a jug and add 1½ times the volume of hot water or stock.

2 Cover the bowl and leave to soak for 5 minutes. Fluff up with a fork before serving.

3 If using for a salad, leave the couscous to cool completely before adding the other salad ingredients.

Bulgur wheat

A form of cracked wheat, bulgur has had some or all of the bran removed. It can be used in salads or served as an accompaniment. It is pre-boiled during manufacturing and may be boiled, steamed or soaked.

Simmering Put the bulgur in a pan and cover with water by about 2.5cm (1in). Bring to the boil, then simmer for 10–15 minutes until just tender. Drain well.

Steaming Line a steamer with a clean teatowel, place the bulgur in the steamer and steam over boiling water for 20 minutes or until the grains are soft.

Soaking Put the bulgur in a deep bowl. Cover with hot water and mix with a fork. Leave to steep for 20 minutes, checking to make sure there is enough water. Drain and fluff up with a fork.

Cooking pasta

When cooking pasta it is not necessary to add oil to the water unless you are cooking filled pasta such as ravioli: the oil will help prevent them from sticking together.

Cooking dried pasta

1 Heat the water with about 1 tsp salt per 100g (3½oz) of pasta. Cover the pan to speed up boiling.

2 When the water has reached a rolling boil, put in all the pasta.

3 Stir well for 30 seconds, to keep the pasta from sticking either to itself or the pan. Once boiling, set the timer for 2 minutes less than the recommended cooking time on the pack and cook uncovered.

4 Check the pasta when the timer goes off, then every 60 seconds until it is cooked al dente: tender with a little bite at the centre. Scoop out a cup of cooking water (it may be useful for loosening up a thick sauce).

5 Drain the pasta well in a colander. Transfer to a serving bowl, and use as required by your recipe.

Cooking fresh pasta

Fresh pasta is cooked in the same way as dried, but for a shorter time.

1 Bring the water to the boil.

2 Add the pasta to the boiling water and stir well. Set the timer for 2 minutes and keep testing every 30 seconds until the pasta is cooked al dente: tender but with a little bite in the centre. Drain as above.

Perfect pasta

- Use about 1 litre (1¾ pints) of water per 100g (3½oz) of pasta.
- Rinse the pasta only if you are going to cool it for use in a salad, then drain well and toss with oil.
- If a recipe calls for cooking the pasta with the sauce after it has boiled, undercook the pasta slightly when boiling it.

Cooking other grains

Quinoa

This nutritious South American grain makes a great alternative to rice.

1   Put the quinoa in a bowl of cold water. Mix well, soak for 2 minutes, then drain. Put in a pan with twice its volume of water. Bring to the boil.

2   Simmer for 10–20 minutes, according to the packet instructions. Remove from the heat, cover and leave to stand for 10 minutes.

Quantities

Allow 50–75g (2–3oz) raw grain per person. Or, if measuring by volume, allow 50–75ml (2–2½fl oz).

Barley

There are three types of barley, all of which may be cooked on their own, or in a soup or stew.

Whole barley Soak the barley overnight in twice its volume of water, then drain well. Put the barley in a heavy-based pan, pour over boiling water and simmer for about 1½ hours or until tender. Check the liquid, adding more if necessary.

Scotch (pot) barley Rinse well, then simmer gently in boiling water for 45–50 minutes until tender.

Pearl barley This barley has had all of its outer husk removed, and needs no soaking. Rinse the barley and put it into a pan with twice its volume of water. Bring to the boil. Turn down the heat and simmer for 25–30 minutes until tender.

Traditional polenta

1 Fill a pan with 1.2 litres (2 pints) water and add ¼ tsp salt. Pour in 225g (8oz) polenta and put the pan over a medium heat.

2 As the water starts to heat up, stir the polenta. Bring to the boil, reduce the heat to a simmer and continue cooking, stirring every few minutes, for 15–20 minutes until it comes away from the sides of the pan.

Cooking polenta

This classic Italian staple made of ground cornmeal may be cooked to make a grainy purée to be served immediately, or cooled and then fried or grilled.

Perfect polenta

- Use coarse cornmeal if you want a slightly gritty texture, or fine cornmeal for a smooth texture.
- If you are serving traditional polenta straight from the pan, have all the other dishes ready – the polenta needs to be eaten straightaway, otherwise it becomes thick and difficult to serve.

Grilling polenta

1 Make traditional polenta (see left), then pour into an oiled baking dish. Smooth the surface with a spatula and leave to cool.

2 Cut the polenta into squares and brush the pieces with olive oil.

3 Preheat the grill or frying pan and cook for 5–10 minutes until hot and browned on both sides.

Baking polenta

1 Preheat the oven to 200°C (180°C fan oven) mark 6. Fill a pan with 1.2 litres (2 pints) water and add ¼ tsp salt. Pour in 225g (8oz) polenta and put it over the heat. Bring to the boil, stirring, then simmer for 5 minutes.

2 Pour the polenta into an oiled baking dish, cover with foil and bake in the oven for 45–50 minutes. Brown under the grill.

Food storage and hygiene

Storing food properly and preparing it in a hygienic way is important to ensure that food remains as nutritious and flavourful as possible, and to reduce the risk of food poisoning.

Hygiene

When you are preparing food, always follow these important guidelines:

Wash your hands thoroughly before handling food and again between handling different types of food, such as raw and cooked meat and poultry. If you have any cuts or grazes on your hands, be sure to keep them covered with a waterproof plaster.

Wash down worksurfaces regularly with a mild detergent solution or multi-surface cleaner.

Use a dishwasher if available. Otherwise, wear rubber gloves for washing-up, so that the water temperature can be hotter than unprotected hands can bear. Change drying-up cloths and cleaning cloths regularly. Note that leaving dishes to drain is more hygienic than drying them with a teatowel.

Keep raw and cooked foods separate, especially meat, fish and poultry. Wash kitchen utensils in between preparing raw and cooked foods. Never put cooked or ready-to-eat foods directly on to a surface that has just had raw fish, meat or poultry on it.

Keep pets out of the kitchen if possible; or make sure they stay away from worksurfaces. Never allow animals on to worksurfaces.

Shopping

Always choose fresh ingredients in prime condition from stores and markets that have a regular turnover of stock to ensure you buy the freshest produce possible.

Make sure items are within their 'best before' or 'use by' date. (Foods with a longer shelf life have a 'best before' date; more perishable items have a 'use by' date.)

Pack frozen and chilled items in an insulated cool bag at the check-out and put them into the freezer or refrigerator as soon as you get home.

During warm weather in particular, buy perishable foods just before you return home. When packing items at the check-out, sort them according to where you will store them when you get home – the refrigerator, freezer, storecupboard, vegetable rack, fruit bowl, etc. This will make unpacking easier – and quicker.

The storecupboard

Although storecupboard ingredients will generally last a long time, correct storage is important:

Always check packaging for storage advice – even with familiar foods, because storage requirements may change if additives, sugar or salt have been reduced.

Check storecupboard foods for their 'best before' or 'use by' date and do not use them if the date has passed.

Keep all food cupboards scrupulously clean and make sure food containers and packets are properly sealed.

Once opened, treat canned foods as though fresh. Always transfer the contents to a clean container, cover and keep in the refrigerator. Similarly, jars, sauce bottles and cartons should be kept chilled after opening. (Check the label for safe storage times after opening.)

Transfer dry goods such as sugar, flour, rice and pasta to moisture-proof containers. When supplies are used up, wash the container well and thoroughly dry before refilling with new supplies.

Store oils in a dark cupboard away from any heat source as heat and light can make them turn rancid and affect their colour. For the same reason, buy olive oil in dark green bottles.

Store vinegars in a cool place; they can turn bad in a warm environment.

Store dried herbs, spices and flavourings in a cool, dark cupboard or in dark jars. Buy in small quantities as their flavour will not last indefinitely.

Refrigerator storage

Fresh food needs to be kept in the cool temperature of the refrigerator to keep it in good condition and discourage the growth of harmful bacteria. Store day-to-day perishable items, such as opened jams and jellies, mayonnaise and bottled sauces, in the refrigerator along with eggs and dairy products, fruit juices, bacon, fresh and cooked meat (on separate shelves), and salads and vegetables (except potatoes, which don't suit being stored in the cold). A refrigerator should be kept at an operating temperature of 4–5°C.

It is worth investing in a refrigerator thermometer to ensure the correct temperature is maintained. To ensure your refrigerator is functioning effectively for safe food storage, follow these guidelines:

To avoid bacterial cross-contamination, store cooked and raw foods on separate shelves, putting cooked foods on the top shelf. Ensure that all items are well wrapped.

into the refrigerator, as this will cause the internal temperature of the refrigerator to rise.

Avoid overfilling the refrigerator, as this restricts the circulation of air and prevents the appliance from working properly.

It can take some time for the refrigerator to return to the correct operating temperature once the door has been opened, so don't leave it open any longer than is necessary.

Clean the refrigerator regularly, using a specially formulated germicidal refrigerator cleaner. Alternatively, use a weak solution of bicarbonate of soda: 1 tbsp to 1 litre (1³/₄ pints) water.

If your refrigerator doesn't have an automatic defrost facility, defrost regularly.

Maximum refrigerator storage times

For pre-packed foods, always adhere to the 'use by' date on the packet. For other foods the following storage times should apply, providing the food is in prime condition when it goes into the refrigerator and that your refrigerator is in good working order:

Vegetables and Fruit

Green vegetables	3–4 days
Salad leaves	2–3 days
Hard and stone fruit	3–7 days
Soft fruit	1–2 days

Dairy Food

Cheese, hard	1 week
Cheese, soft	2–3 days
Eggs	1 week
Milk	4–5 days

Soups

Cook's Tip

To make a bouquet garni, tie together a sprig each of thyme and parsley with a bay leaf and a piece of celery.

French Onion Soup

75g (3oz) butter

700g (1½lb) small onions, finely chopped

3 garlic cloves, crushed

1 tbsp plain flour

200ml (7fl oz) dry white wine

1.5 litres (2½ pints) vegetable stock

bouquet garni (see Cook's Tip)

salt and ground black pepper

1 small baguette, cut into slices 1cm (½in) thick, to serve

50g (2oz) Gruyère cheese or Cheddar, grated, to serve

1 Melt the butter in a large heavy-based pan. Add the onions and cook slowly over a very low heat, stirring frequently, until very soft and golden brown; this should take at least 30 minutes. Add the garlic and flour and cook, stirring, for 1 minute.

2 Pour in the wine and let bubble until reduced by half. Add the stock, bouquet garni and seasoning. Bring to the boil and simmer gently, uncovered, for 20–30 minutes.

3 Discard the bouquet garni and let the soup cool a little. Put one third into a blender or food processor and purée until smooth, then stir this back into the soup in the pan.

4 Preheat the grill. Lightly toast the slices of French bread on both sides. Reheat the soup and adjust the seasoning.

5 Divide the soup among four ovenproof soup bowls. Float two or three slices of toast on each portion and sprinkle thickly with the grated cheese. Stand the bowls under a hot grill until the cheese has melted and turned golden brown. Serve at once.

Serves 4	EASY		NUTRITIONAL INFORMATION
	Preparation Time 30 minutes	**Cooking Time** about 1 hour	**Per Serving** 438 calories, 21.2g fat (of which 13.2g saturates), 45.4g carbohydrate, 1.3g salt

Easy Pea Soup

1 small baguette, thinly sliced

2 tbsp basil-infused olive oil, plus extra to drizzle

450g (1lb) frozen peas, thawed

600ml (1 pint) vegetable stock

salt and ground black pepper

1 Preheat the oven to 220°C (200°C fan oven) mark 7. To make the croûtes, put the bread on a baking sheet, drizzle with 2 tbsp oil and bake for 10–15 minutes until golden.

2 Meanwhile, put the peas in a food processor, add the stock and season with salt and pepper. Blend for 2–3 minutes.

3 Pour the soup into a pan and bring to the boil, then reduce the heat and simmer for 10 minutes. Spoon into warmed bowls, add the croûtes, drizzle with extra oil and sprinkle with salt and pepper. Serve immediately.

Serves 4	EASY		NUTRITIONAL INFORMATION	
	Preparation Time 2 minutes, plus thawing	**Cooking Time** 15 minutes	**Per Serving** 408 calories, 9g fat (of which 2g saturates), 69g carbohydrate, 1.8g salt	Dairy free

Cook's Tips

Chillies vary enormously in strength, from quite mild to blisteringly hot, depending on the type of chilli and its ripeness. Taste a small piece first to check it's not too hot for you. To prepare, see page 15.

Be extremely careful when handling chillies not to touch or rub your eyes with your fingers, as they will sting. Wash knives immediately after handling chillies. As a precaution, use rubber gloves when preparing them if you like.

Sweet Potato Soup

1 tbsp olive oil

1 large onion, finely chopped

2 tsp coriander seeds, crushed

2 fresh red chillies, seeded and chopped (see Cook's Tips)

1 butternut squash, about 750g (1lb 11oz), peeled and roughly chopped

2 sweet potatoes, roughly chopped

2 tomatoes, peeled and diced

1.7 litres (3 pints) hot vegetable stock

salt and ground black pepper

cheese straws to serve

1 Heat the oil in a large pan over a gentle heat and fry the onion for about 10 minutes until soft. Add the coriander seeds and chillies to the pan and cook for 1–2 minutes.

2 Add the squash, sweet potatoes and tomatoes and cook for 5 minutes. Add the hot stock, cover and bring to the boil. Simmer gently for 15 minutes or until the vegetables are soft. Using a blender, purée the soup in batches until smooth. Season with salt and pepper. Reheat gently, then divide among eight warmed bowls. Sprinkle with black pepper and serve with cheese straws.

EASY		NUTRITIONAL INFORMATION		Serves
Preparation Time 20 minutes	**Cooking Time** 35 minutes	**Per Serving** 78 calories, 2g fat (of which trace saturates), 14g carbohydrate, 0.8g salt	Dairy free	**8**

Mixed Mushroom Soup

15g (½oz) dried porcini mushrooms

1 tbsp sunflower oil, plus 50ml (2fl oz) to shallow-fry

1 small onion, chopped

450g (1lb) chestnut mushrooms, chopped

600ml (1 pint) hot vegetable stock

2 slices white bread, crusts removed, cut into cubes

2 garlic cloves, finely sliced

salt and ground black pepper

freshly chopped flat-leafed parsley to garnish

1 Put the porcini in a bowl, pour 75ml (2½fl oz) boiling water over them and leave to soak for 10 minutes. Strain the porcini, put the liquid to one side, then chop roughly, keeping 1 tbsp to use as a garnish.

2 Heat 1 tbsp oil in a pan. Add the onion and porcini and cook over a medium heat for 5 minutes. Add the chestnut mushrooms, increase the heat and brown lightly for 5 minutes. Add the reserved porcini liquid and the stock, then bring to the boil. Season well with salt and pepper and simmer for 20 minutes.

3 To make croûtons, heat 50ml (2fl oz) oil in a frying pan. Add the bread and garlic and stir-fry for 2 minutes until golden. Drain on kitchen paper.

4 Take the soup off the heat and leave to cool slightly. Purée in a blender until smooth, then transfer to a clean pan. Reheat gently, then divide among four warmed bowls. Serve topped with the croûtons, reserved porcini and a sprinkling of parsley.

Serves 4	EASY		NUTRITIONAL INFORMATION	
	Preparation Time 15 minutes, plus soaking	**Cooking Time** 35 minutes	**Per Serving** 158 calories, 11.9g fat (of which 1.5g saturates), 9.5g carbohydrate, 0.2g salt	Dairy free

Leek and Potato Soup

25g (1oz) butter
1 onion, finely chopped
1 garlic clove, crushed
550g (1¼lb) leeks, chopped
200g (7oz) floury potatoes, sliced
1.3 litres (2¼ pints) hot vegetable stock
crème fraîche and chopped chives to garnish

1 Melt the butter in a pan over a gentle heat, and cook the onion for 10–15 minutes until soft. Add the garlic and cook for a further minute. Add the leeks and cook for 5–10 minutes until softened. Add the potatoes and toss together with the leeks.

2 Pour in the hot stock and bring to the boil. Simmer the soup for 20 minutes until the potatoes are tender. Cool a little, then purée in a food processor.

3 Reheat gently and serve garnished with crème fraîche and chives.

EASY		NUTRITIONAL INFORMATION	Serves
Preparation Time 10 minutes	**Cooking Time** 45 minutes	**Per Serving** 117 calories, 6g fat (of which 4g saturates), 13g carbohydrate, 0.1g salt	**4**

Freezing Tip

To freeze Freeze the soup in a sealed container at step 2. It will keep for up to three months.
To use Thaw in the fridge overnight. Reheat gently and simmer over a low heat for 5 minutes.

Beetroot Soup

1 tbsp olive oil

1 onion, finely chopped

750g (1lb 11oz) raw beetroot, peeled and cut into 1cm (½in) cubes

275g (10oz) potatoes, roughly chopped

2 litres (3½ pints) hot vegetable stock

juice of 1 lemon

8 tbsp soured cream

50g (2oz) mixed root vegetable crisps

salt and ground black pepper

2 tbsp chopped chives to garnish

1 Heat the oil in a large pan, add the onion and cook for 5 minutes. Add the beetroot and potatoes and cook for a further 5 minutes.

2 Add the stock and lemon juice, then bring to the boil. Season with salt and pepper, reduce the heat and simmer, half-covered, for 25 minutes. Cool slightly, then purée in a blender until smooth.

3 Pour the soup into a clean pan and reheat gently. Divide the soup among eight warmed bowls. Add 1 tbsp soured cream to each bowl, sprinkle with black pepper and top with a few vegetable crisps and sprinkle the chopped chives on top to serve.

Serves 8	EASY		NUTRITIONAL INFORMATION
	Preparation Time 15 minutes	**Cooking Time** 40–45 minutes	**Per Serving** 216 calories, 9g fat (of which 3g saturates), 31g carbohydrate, 1.5g salt

2 tbsp olive oil

1 small onion, finely chopped

1 carrot, chopped

1 celery stick, chopped

1 garlic clove, crushed

2 tbsp chopped fresh thyme

1 litre (1¾ pints) vegetable stock

400g can chopped tomatoes

400g can borlotti beans, drained and rinsed

125g (4oz) minestrone pasta

175g (6oz) shredded Savoy cabbage, shredded

salt and ground black pepper

fresh ready-made pesto, toasted ciabatta and extra virgin olive oil, to serve

Quick Winter Minestrone

1 Heat the olive oil in a large pan and add the onion, carrot and celery. Cook for 8–10 minutes until softened, then add the garlic and thyme. Fry for another 2–3 minutes.

2 Add the stock, tomatoes and half the borlotti beans. Mash the remaining beans, stir into the soup and simmer for 30 minutes, adding the minestrone pasta and cabbage for the last 10 minutes of cooking time.

3 Check the seasoning and correct, if necessary, then serve the soup with a dollop of fresh pesto on top and slices of toasted ciabatta drizzled with extra virgin olive oil on the side.

EASY		NUTRITIONAL INFORMATION		Serves
Preparation Time 10 minutes	**Cooking Time** 45 minutes	**Per Serving** 334 calories, 11.2g fat (of which 2.5g saturates), 46.8g carbohydrate, 1.5g salt	Dairy free	**4**

Cauliflower Soup

2 x 400ml cans coconut milk

750ml (1¼ pints) vegetable stock

4 garlic cloves, finely chopped

5cm (2in) piece fresh root ginger, peeled and finely chopped

4 lemongrass stalks, roughly chopped

4 red chillies, seeded and chopped (see page 35)

4 kaffir lime leaves, shredded (optional)

2 tbsp groundnut oil

2 tsp sesame oil

1 large onion, thinly sliced

2 tsp ground turmeric

2 tsp sugar

900g (2lb) cauliflower florets

2 tbsp lime juice

2 tbsp light soy sauce

4 spring onions, shredded

4 tbsp freshly chopped coriander

salt and ground black pepper

1 Put the coconut milk and stock into a pan. Add the garlic and ginger with the lemongrass, chillies and lime leaves. Bring to the boil, cover and simmer for 15 minutes. Strain and keep the liquid to one side.

2 Heat the oils together in a clean pan. Add the onion, turmeric and sugar and fry gently for 5 minutes. Add the cauliflower to the pan and stir-fry for 5 minutes or until lightly golden.

3 Add the reserved liquid, the lime juice and soy sauce. Bring to the boil, then cover and simmer for 10–15 minutes until the cauliflower is tender. Season with salt and pepper, then divide among six warmed bowls. Scatter the spring onions and coriander on top and serve.

EASY		NUTRITIONAL INFORMATION		Serves
Preparation Time 25 minutes	**Cooking Time** 40 minutes	**Per Serving** 115 calories, 6.5g fat (of which 1.1g saturates), 18.2g carbohydrate, 1.1g salt	Dairy free	**6**

Bloody Mary Soup with Bruschetta

700g (1½lb) ripe plum tomatoes, thinly sliced

6 spring onions, trimmed and finely chopped

grated zest of ½ lemon

2 tbsp freshly chopped basil

125ml (4fl oz) extra virgin olive oil, plus extra to drizzle

2 tbsp balsamic vinegar

2–3 garlic cloves, crushed

a pinch of sugar

60ml (2fl oz) chilled vodka

a few drops of Tabasco

150ml (5fl oz) tomato juice

8 thin slices of bruschetta

salt and ground black pepper

fresh basil leaves to garnish

1 Put the tomatoes in a large shallow dish and scatter with the spring onions, lemon zest and basil.

2 Blend together the oil, vinegar, 1 crushed garlic clove, the sugar, vodka, Worcestershire sauce and Tabasco. Season to taste with salt and pepper and pour over the tomatoes. Cover and leave to marinate for 2 hours at room temperature.

3 Put the tomato salad and tomato juice in a blender and purée until very smooth. Transfer to a bowl and leave to chill in the fridge for 1 hour.

4 Just before serving, preheat the grill. Put the bread on the grill rack and toast lightly on both sides. Rub each one with the remaining crushed garlic, drizzle with oil and garnish with fresh basil leaves. Spoon the soup into serving bowls, drizzle with oil, sprinkle with black pepper and serve at once with the bruschetta.

Cook's Tip

- -

This recipe is not suitable for children because it contains alcohol.

Serves	EASY		NUTRITIONAL INFORMATION	
4	**Preparation Time** 15 minutes, plus marinating and chilling	**Cooking Time** 5 minutes	**Per Serving** 468 calories, 22.8g fat (of which 3.5g saturates), 51.9g carbohydrate, 1.5g salt	Dairy free

Cook's Tip

Parmesan Crisps make great cocktail nibbles, or can be served with soups or to garnish salads or pasta. Preheat the oven to 200°C (180°C fan oven) mark 6 and line two baking sheets with baking parchment. Grate 125g (4oz) Parmesan. Put heaped tablespoons of Parmesan on the sheets, evenly spaced, and spread each one out slightly. Sprinkle ½ tsp poppy seeds over them. Bake for 5–10 minutes until lacy and golden. Leave on the tray to cool and firm up slightly, then transfer to a wire rack.

Creamy Watercress Soup

Try Something Different

Use spinach instead of watercress.

250g (9oz) watercress

50g (2oz) butter

1 onion, finely chopped

700g (1½lb) potatoes, cut into small pieces

900ml (1½ pints) milk

900ml (1½ pints) vegetable stock

6 tbsp single cream

salt and ground black pepper

Parmesan Crisps to serve (see Cook's Tip)

1 Trim the watercress and discard any coarse stalks. Reserve a few sprigs for the garnish and chop the rest roughly.

2 Melt the butter in a large pan, add the onion and cook gently for 8–10 minutes until soft. Add the potatoes and cook for 1 minute, then pour in the milk and stock and bring to the boil. Reduce the heat and cook for 15–20 minutes until tender.

3 Take the pan off the heat. Stir in the watercress, then transfer to a blender and process in batches until smooth. Pour the soup back into a clean pan.

4 Add the cream and season to taste. Heat through and garnish with the reserved watercress sprigs. Serve with Parmesan Crisps, if you like.

Serves	EASY		NUTRITIONAL INFORMATION
6	**Preparation Time** 15 minutes	**Cooking Time** 30 minutes	**Per Serving** 263 calories, 13.1g fat (of which 8g saturates), 29.7g carbohydrate, 0.5g salt

Cook's Tip

Pistou is a Provençal condiment similar to Italian pesto. To make your own, use a pestle and mortar, or a small bowl and the end of a rolling pin, or a food processor. Pound together ¾ tsp sea salt and 6 chopped garlic cloves until smooth. Add 15g (½oz) chopped fresh basil and pound to a paste, then mix in 12 tbsp olive oil, a little at a time. Store in a sealed jar in the refrigerator. It will keep for up to one week.

Summer Vegetable Soup with Herb Pistou

3 tbsp sunflower oil

1 onion, finely chopped

225g (8oz) waxy potatoes, peeled and finely diced

175g (6oz) carrots, peeled and finely diced

1 medium turnip, peeled and finely diced

4 bay leaves

6 large fresh sage leaves

2 courgettes, about 375g (13oz), finely diced

175g (6oz) green beans, trimmed and halved

125g (4oz) shelled small peas

225g (8oz) tomatoes, seeded and finely diced

1 small broccoli head, broken into florets

salt and ground black pepper

Pistou (see Cook's Tip) or ready-made pesto to serve

1 Heat the oil in a large pan over a gentle heat. Add the onion, potatoes, carrots and turnip and cook for 10 minutes. Pour in 1.7 litres (3 pints) cold water, season with salt and pepper, bring to the boil and add the bay and sage leaves. Simmer for 25 minutes.

2 Add the courgettes, beans, peas and tomatoes. Bring back to the boil and simmer for 10–15 minutes. Add the broccoli 5 minutes before the end of the cooking time.

3 Remove the bay and sage leaves and adjust the seasoning. Pour the soup into warmed bowls and serve immediately; serve the pistou or pesto separately to stir into the hot soup.

EASY		NUTRITIONAL INFORMATION		Serves
Preparation Time 20 minutes	**Cooking Time** about 1 hour	**Per Serving** 163 calories, 7g fat (of which 1g saturates), 17g carbohydrate, 0.1g salt	Dairy free	**6**

Cucumber, Yogurt and Mint Soup

1 cucumber, coarsely grated
500g (1lb 2oz) Greek yogurt
a generous handful of mint leaves, chopped
1 large garlic clove, crushed
125ml (4fl oz) cold water or light vegetable stock
salt and ground black pepper
6 ice cubes and mint sprigs to serve

1 Set aside 6 tbsp of the grated cucumber. Put the remainder in a large bowl with all the remaining ingredients for the soup and mix together. Chill for up to 12 hours.

2 Before serving, stir the soup, then taste and adjust the seasoning. Spoon the soup into six bowls and drop an ice cube, 1 tbsp of the reserved cucumber and a few mint sprigs into each bowl.

Serves	EASY		NUTRITIONAL INFORMATION
6	**Preparation Time** 15 minutes, plus chilling		**Per Serving** 105 calories, 9g fat (of which 4g saturates), 3g carbohydrate, 0.5g salt

Try Something Different

- -

Add a bruised lemongrass stalk to the soup in place of the bay leaf to impart a delicate flavour and fragrance. To bruise lemongrass, press it firmly under the blade of a heavy flat knife.

75g (3oz) butter

2 onions, thinly sliced

450g (1lb) leeks (white part only), sliced

175g (6oz) floury potatoes, peeled and diced

1 bay leaf

1.3 litres (2¼ pints) vegetable stock

300ml (½ pint) semi-skimmed milk

150ml (¼ pint) crème fraîche

salt and white pepper

extra crème fraîche and snipped chives to serve

Vichyssoise

1 Melt the butter in a large pan and add the onions and leeks. Stir well, add 3 tbsp water, cover tightly and sweat over a gentle heat for 10 minutes until soft and golden.

2 Stir in the diced potatoes, bay leaf, stock and milk. Bring to the boil, then lower the heat, cover and simmer for 20 minutes until the potatoes are tender.

3 Discard the bay leaf. Leave the soup to cool a little, then transfer to a blender or food processor and purée until smooth. Pass through a sieve. Return to the pan if serving hot.

4 Stir in the crème fraîche and season with salt and pepper to taste. Either cool and chill (in this case, season liberally) or reheat and pour into warmed soup bowls. Serve topped with a dollop of crème fraîche and chives.

EASY		NUTRITIONAL INFORMATION		Serves
Preparation Time 15 minutes, plus optional chilling	**Cooking Time** 30 minutes	**Per Serving** 271 calories, 21.7g fat (of which 14.1g saturates), 15.2g carbohydrate, 0.3g salt	Gluten free	**6**

Carrot and Coriander Soup

40g (1½oz) butter
175g (6oz) leeks, sliced
450g (1lb) carrots, sliced
2 tsp ground coriander
1 tsp plain flour
1.2 litres (2 pints) vegetable stock
150ml (¼ pint) single cream
salt and ground black pepper
coriander leaves, roughly torn, to serve

1 Melt the butter in a large pan. Add the leeks and carrots, stir, then cover the pan and cook gently for 7–10 minutes until the vegetables begin to soften but not colour.

2 Stir in the ground coriander and flour and cook, stirring, for 1 minute.

3 Add the stock and bring to the boil, stirring. Season, then reduce the heat, cover and simmer for about 20 minutes, until the vegetables are tender.

4 Allow to cool a little, then purée in a blender or food processor until quite smooth.

5 Return to the pan and stir in the cream. Adjust the seasoning and reheat gently; do not boil. Serve scattered with torn coriander leaves.

EASY		NUTRITIONAL INFORMATION	Serves
Preparation Time 15 minutes	**Cooking Time** about 30 minutes	**Per Serving** 140 calories, 10.6g fat (of which 6.7g saturates), 9.7g carbohydrate, 0.2g salt	**6**

2

Salads

Asparagus, Pea and Mint Rice Salad

175g (6oz) mixed basmati and wild rice

1 large shallot, finely sliced

grated zest and juice of 1 small lemon

2 tbsp sunflower oil

12 fresh mint leaves, roughly chopped, plus extra sprigs to garnish

150g (5oz) asparagus tips

75g (3oz) fresh or frozen peas

salt and ground black pepper

1 Put the rice in a pan with twice its volume of water and a pinch of salt. Cover and bring to the boil. Reduce the heat to very low and cook according to the packet instructions. Once cooked, tip the rice on to a baking sheet and spread out to cool quickly. When cool, spoon into a large bowl.

2 In a small bowl, mix the shallot with the lemon zest and juice, oil and chopped mint, then stir into the rice. Season with salt and pepper.

3 Bring a large pan of lightly salted water to the boil. Add the asparagus and peas and cook for 3–4 minutes until tender. Drain and refresh in a bowl of cold water. Drain well and stir into the rice. Put into a serving dish and garnish with mint sprigs.

Serves 6	EASY		NUTRITIONAL INFORMATION	
	Preparation Time 10 minutes	**Cooking Time** 20 minutes	**Per Serving** 157 calories, 4g fat (of which trace saturates), 26g carbohydrate, trace salt	Gluten free Dairy free

Try Something Different

Use parsley instead of basil, and add 4 finely chopped
spring onions.
Scatter the salad with 2 tbsp lightly toasted pumpkin seeds
or sunflower seeds.

250g (9oz) cooked beetroot (without vinegar),
roughly chopped

400g can chickpeas, drained and rinsed

50g (2oz) sultanas

20g (³⁄₄oz) fresh basil

1 medium carrot, peeled and grated

½ small white cabbage, finely shredded

juice of ½ lemon

150g (5oz) Greek yogurt

20g (³⁄₄oz) fresh mint, finely chopped

2 tbsp extra virgin olive oil

salt and ground black pepper

Chickpea and Beetroot Salad

1 Put the beetroot and chickpeas in a large bowl. Add
the sultanas, tear the basil and add, then add the
carrot, cabbage and lemon juice.

2 Put the yogurt in a separate bowl. Add the mint and
oil and season with salt and pepper. Spoon on to the
salad and mix everything together. Serve immediately.

EASY	NUTRITIONAL INFORMATION		Serves
Preparation Time 15 minutes	**Per Serving** 266 calories, 12g fat (of which 3g saturates), 32g carbohydrate, 0.7g salt	Gluten free	**4**

Try Something Different

Use papaya instead of mango.
Ginger and Chilli Dressing: Mix together 2 tsp grated fresh root ginger, 1 tbsp sweet chilli sauce, 2 tsp white wine vinegar and 2 tbsp walnut oil. Season with salt.
Peanut Dressing: Mix together 1 tbsp peanut butter, ¼ of a whole dried chilli, crushed, 4 tsp white wine vinegar, 3 tbsp walnut oil, 1 tsp sesame oil and a dash of soy sauce.

Sprouted Bean and Mango Salad

3 tbsp mango chutney

grated zest and juice of 1 lime

2 tbsp olive oil

4 plum tomatoes

1 small red onion, finely chopped

1 red pepper, seeded and finely diced

1 yellow pepper, seeded and finely diced

1 mango, finely diced

4 tbsp freshly chopped coriander

150g (5oz) sprouted beans

salt and ground black pepper

1 To make the dressing, put the mango chutney in a small bowl and add the lime zest and juice. Whisk in the oil and season with salt and pepper.

2 Quarter the tomatoes, discard the seeds and then dice. Put into a large bowl with the onion, peppers, mango, coriander and sprouted beans. Pour in the dressing and mix well. Serve immediately.

Serves	EASY		NUTRITIONAL INFORMATION	
6	**Preparation Time** 15 minutes		**Per Serving** 103 calories, 4g fat (of which 1g saturates), 15g carbohydrate, 0.1g salt	Gluten free Dairy free

Cook's Tip

Panzanella is a Tuscan salad, which uses stale bread.

Get Ahead

This salad is best made two or three hours ahead to let the flavours mingle.

Panzanella

2–3 thick slices from a day-old country loaf, about 100g (3½oz), torn or cut into cubes

450g (1lb) ripe tomatoes, roughly chopped

2 tbsp capers

1 tsp freshly chopped thyme

1 small red onion, thinly sliced

2 garlic cloves, finely chopped

2 small red chillies, seeded and finely chopped (see page 35)

4 tbsp extra virgin olive oil

125g (4oz) pitted black olives

50g (2oz) sun-dried tomatoes, roughly chopped

8 fresh basil leaves

25g (1oz) Parmesan, pared into shavings with a vegetable peeler

salt and ground black pepper

fresh thyme sprigs to garnish

1 Put the bread in a large bowl with the tomatoes, capers, thyme, onion, garlic, chillies, oil, olives and sun-dried tomatoes. Season well with salt and pepper, then toss together and leave in a cool place for at least 30 minutes.

2 Toss the salad thoroughly again. Tear the basil into pieces and scatter over the salad with the Parmesan shavings. Garnish with thyme sprigs, and then serve.

EASY	NUTRITIONAL INFORMATION	Serves
Preparation Time 20 minutes, plus minimum 30 minutes chilling	**Per Serving** 228 calories, 14g fat (of which 3g saturates), 21g carbohydrate, 0.6g salt	**4**

Guacamole Salad

3 beef tomatoes, each sliced horizontally into six

½ small onion, finely sliced

1 garlic clove, crushed

1 tbsp fresh coriander leaves, plus extra sprigs to garnish

4 ripe avocados

juice of 1 lime

200g (7oz) feta cheese, crumbled

100g (3½oz) sunblush tomatoes in oil

salt and ground black pepper

lime wedges to serve

1 Divide the tomato slices among six serving plates, then scatter the onion, garlic and coriander leaves over them.

2 Cut each avocado into quarters as far as the stone. Keeping the avocado whole, start at the pointed end and peel away the skin. Separate each quarter, remove the stone, then slice the pieces lengthways. Squeeze the lime juice over the slices to stop them from browning and arrange on the plates.

3 Top with the feta cheese, sunblush tomatoes and a sprig of coriander. Finish each salad with a drizzling of oil reserved from the sunblush tomatoes and season well with salt and pepper. Serve with lime wedges.

Serves	EASY		NUTRITIONAL INFORMATION	
6	**Preparation Time** 15 minutes	**Cooking Time** 20 minutes	**Per Serving** 317 calories, 28g fat (of which 9g saturates), 7g carbohydrate, 1.3g salt	Gluten free

Cook's Tip

Halloumi is a firm cheese made from ewe's milk. It is best used sliced and cooked.

Halloumi and Avocado Salad

250g (9oz) halloumi cheese, sliced into eight (see Cook's Tip)

1 tbsp flour, seasoned

2 tbsp olive oil

200g (7oz) mixed leaf salad

2 ripe avocados, halved, stoned, peeled and sliced

fresh rocket leaves to garnish

lemon halves to serve

For the mint dressing

3 tbsp lemon juice

8 tbsp olive oil

3 tbsp freshly chopped mint

salt and ground black pepper

1 To make the dressing, whisk the lemon juice with the oil and mint, then season with salt and pepper.

2 Coat the halloumi with the flour. Heat the oil in a large frying pan and fry the cheese for 1 minute on each side or until it forms a golden crust.

3 Meanwhile, in a large bowl, add half the dressing to the salad leaves and avocado and toss together. Arrange the hot cheese on top and drizzle the remaining dressing over it. Garnish with rocket leaves and serve with lemon halves to squeeze over the salad.

Serves	EASY		NUTRITIONAL INFORMATION
4	**Preparation Time** 10 minutes	**Cooking Time** 2 minutes	**Per Serving** 397 calories, 34g fat (of which 13g saturates), 11g carbohydrate, 2.3g salt

Cannellini Bean and Sunblush Tomato Salad

½ red onion, very finely sliced

2 tbsp red wine vinegar

a small handful each of freshly chopped mint and flat-leafed parsley

2 x 400g cans cannellini beans, drained and rinsed

4 tbsp extra virgin olive oil

4 celery sticks, sliced

75g (3oz) sunblush tomatoes, snipped in half

salt and ground black pepper

1 Put the onion into a small bowl, add the vinegar and toss. Leave to marinate for 30 minutes – this stage is important as it takes the astringency out of the onion.

2 Tip the onion and vinegar into a large bowl, add the remaining ingredients, season with salt and pepper and toss everything together.

EASY	NUTRITIONAL INFORMATION		Serves
Preparation Time 5 minutes, plus 30 minutes marinating	**Per Serving** 163 calories, 8g fat (of which 1g saturates), 17g carbohydrate, 1.3g salt	Gluten free Dairy free	**6**

Warm Tofu, Fennel and Bean Salad

1 tbsp olive oil, plus 1 tsp

1 red onion, finely sliced

1 fennel bulb, finely sliced

1 tbsp cider vinegar

400g can butter beans, drained and rinsed

2 tbsp freshly chopped flat-leafed parsley

200g (7oz) smoked tofu

salt and ground black pepper

1 Heat 1 tbsp oil in a large frying pan. Add the onion and fennel and cook over a medium heat for 5–10 minutes until soft.

2 Add the cider vinegar and heat through for 2 minutes. Stir in the butter beans and parsley, season with salt and pepper, then tip into a bowl.

3 Slice the smoked tofu horizontally into four and then into eight triangles. Add to the pan with the remaining 1tsp oil. Cook for 2 minutes on each side or until golden.

4 Divide the bean mixture among four plates, then add two slices of tofu to each plate.

Serves	EASY			NUTRITIONAL INFORMATION	
4	**Preparation Time** 10 minutes	**Cooking Time** 15 minutes		**Per Serving** 150 calories, 6g fat (of which 1g saturates), 15g carbohydrate, 0.8g salt	Gluten free Dairy free

Red Onion and Gorgonzola Salad

1½ tbsp olive oil

4 red onions, about 500g (1lb 2oz) total weight, peeled but with root intact, cut into wedges

1 tbsp soft light brown sugar

2½ tbsp balsamic vinegar

350g (12oz) mixed salad leaves, washed and dried

275g (10oz) Gorgonzola, crumbled

For the dressing

1 tbsp clear honey

1 tsp Dijon mustard

3 tbsp red wine vinegar

9 tbsp extra virgin olive oil

salt and ground black pepper

1 Heat the oil in a large frying pan. Add the onion wedges in a single layer, cover with a lid and cook over a low to moderate heat for 15 minutes or until the onions have softened and are beginning to brown on the underside.

2 Sprinkle the sugar over the onions, cover the pan and cook for a further 10 minutes until the exposed side starts to caramelise. Add the balsamic vinegar and cook, uncovered, until most of the vinegar has evaporated and the onions are sticky.

3 To make the dressing, put the honey, mustard, vinegar and oil in a bowl. Season to taste with salt and pepper and whisk together.

4 Put the salad leaves in a large bowl with the onions and cheese and toss gently to mix. Divide among eight plates, then pour the dressing over the salad and serve immediately.

EASY		NUTRITIONAL INFORMATION		Serves
Preparation Time 15 minutes	**Cooking Time** 30 minutes	**Per Serving** 284 calories, 24g fat (of which 9g saturates), 9g carbohydrate, 1.2g salt	Gluten free	**8**

Warm Pear and Walnut Caesar Salad

50g (2oz) walnut pieces

1 tbsp walnut or mild olive oil

small knob of butter

3 firm rosy pears, peeled, quartered, cored and thickly sliced

1 bag Caesar salad with croûtons, dressing and Parmesan

100g (3½oz) blue cheese, such as Roquefort, Stilton or Danish blue, crumbled

1 bunch of chives, roughly chopped, to garnish

1 Put the walnuts in a non-stick frying pan and dry-fry over a medium heat for about 1 minute until lightly toasted. Set aside.

2 Heat the oil and butter in the pan, then add the pears. Fry for 2 minutes on each side or until golden. Remove with a slotted spoon.

3 To serve, put the salad leaves into a large bowl. Add the walnuts, pears, croûtons, Parmesan and blue cheese. Add the salad dressing and toss lightly, or serve the dressing separately in a small bowl. Serve immediately, garnished with chives.

Get Ahead

Complete the recipe up to the end of step 2, then leave the pears in the frying pan and set aside for up to 4 hours.

To use Warm the pears in the pan for 1 minute, then complete the recipe.

EASY		NUTRITIONAL INFORMATION	Serves
Preparation Time 10 minutes	**Cooking Time** 5 minutes	**Per Serving** 397 calories, 31g fat (of which 8g saturates), 19g carbohydrate, 1.3g salt	6

Griddled Polenta with Gorgonzola Salad

2 tbsp olive oil, plus extra to grease

300ml (½ pint) semi-skimmed milk

10 sage leaves, roughly chopped

125g (4oz) quick-cook polenta (see page 26)

2 garlic cloves, crushed

25g (1oz) butter

100g (3½oz) salad leaves

125g (4oz) Gorgonzola, cut into cubes

125g (4oz) each sunblush tomatoes and roasted red peppers

salt and ground black pepper

1 Lightly oil a 450g (1lb) loaf tin. Put the milk in a pan, then add the sage, 1 scant tsp salt and 300ml (½ pint) water and bring to the boil. Add the polenta to the pan in a thin, steady stream, stirring, to make a smooth paste.

2 Reduce the heat, add the garlic and cook for about 8 minutes, stirring occasionally. Add the oil, then season with pepper and stir well. Press into the prepared loaf tin, smooth the top and leave to cool for 45 minutes.

3 Once the polenta is cool, turn out on to a board and cut into eight slices.

4 Melt the butter in a griddle pan and fry the polenta slices on each side until golden. Divide among four plates. Add the salad leaves, Gorgonzola, sunblush tomatoes and peppers and serve.

Serves	EASY		NUTRITIONAL INFORMATION	
4	**Preparation Time** 20 minutes, plus 45 minutes cooling	**Cooking Time** 20 minutes	**Per Serving** 362 calories, 22g fat (of which 11g saturates), 28g carbohydrate, 1.1g salt	Gluten free

½ tbsp ground cumin

½ tsp ground cinnamon

2 tbsp sunflower oil

2 large red onions, sliced

250g (9oz) basmati rice

600ml (1 pint) hot vegetable stock

400g can lentils, drained and rinsed

salt and ground black pepper

For the salad

75g (3oz) watercress

250g (9oz) broccoli, steamed and chopped into 2.5cm (1in) pieces

25g (1oz) sultanas

75g (3oz) chopped dried apricots, chopped

75g (3oz) mixed nuts and seeds

2 tbsp freshly chopped flat-leafed parsley

100g (3½oz) goat's cheese, crumbled

Warm Spiced Rice Salad

1 Put the cumin and cinnamon into a large, deep frying pan and heat gently for 1–2 minutes. Add the oil and onions and fry over a low heat for 8–10 minutes until the onion is soft and golden. Add the rice, toss to coat in the spices and onions, then add the stock. Cover and cook for 12–15 minutes until the stock is absorbed and the rice is cooked. Season, tip into a serving bowl and add the lentils.

2 To make the salad, add the watercress, broccoli, sultanas, apricots, and mixed nuts and seeds to the bowl. Scatter with the parsley, then toss together, top with the cheese and serve immediately.

EASY		NUTRITIONAL INFORMATION		Serves
Preparation Time 10 minutes	**Cooking Time** 20–30 minutes	**Per Serving** 700 calories, 27g fat (of which 6g saturates), 88g carbohydrate, 0.7g salt	Gluten free	**4**

Cook's Tip

Find marinated artichokes in supermarkets; alternatively, buy canned artichoke hearts, drain, slice and cover in olive oil. They will keep in the refrigerator for up to one week.

Grilled Ciabatta and Mozzarella Salad

8 thick slices Italian bread, such as ciabatta

2 tsp olive paste or sun-dried tomato paste

2 x 150g packs mozzarella cheese, drained and sliced

4 tbsp olive oil, plus extra to drizzle

2 tbsp balsamic vinegar

280g jar artichoke hearts in oil, drained and sliced (see Cook's Tip)

100g (3½oz) rocket salad

50g (2oz) sun-dried tomato halves

salt and ground black pepper

1 Toast the bread slices on one side. Spread the untoasted side with olive or sun-dried tomato paste, then top with mozzarella slices and drizzle lightly with oil.

2 Put the vinegar in a bowl, season and whisk in the 4 tbsp oil. Add the artichoke hearts.

3 Place the bread slices under a preheated grill for 2–3 minutes or until the mozzarella browns lightly.

4 Toss the rocket salad with the artichoke mixture and divide among four plates. Top with two slices of grilled bread and the sun-dried tomatoes and serve.

Serves 4	EASY		NUTRITIONAL INFORMATION
	Preparation Time 10 minutes	**Cooking Time** 5 minutes	**Per Serving** 613 calories, 33g fat (of which 13g saturates), 56g carbohydrate, 2.4g salt

Cook's Tip

To prepare fresh broad beans, first remove the beans from their pods. Cook in boiling water for 2 minutes, then drain and plunge into cold water. Squeeze gently to pop the beans out of their skins – either eat cold or reheat briefly in boiling water.

Warm Broad Bean and Feta Salad

225g (8oz) broad beans, frozen, thawed or canned –
if using fresh beans you will need to start with
700g (1½lb) pods (see Cook's Tip)
100g (3½oz) feta cheese, chopped
2 tbsp freshly chopped mint
2 tbsp extra virgin olive oil
a squeeze of lemon juice
salt and ground black pepper
lemon wedges to serve

1 Cook the beans in lightly salted boiling water for 3–5 minutes until tender. Drain, then plunge into cold water and drain again.

2 Tip the beans into a bowl, add the feta, mint and oil and a squeeze of lemon juice. Season well and toss together. Serve with lemon wedges.

EASY		NUTRITIONAL INFORMATION		Serves
Preparation Time 15 minutes	**Cooking Time** 3–5 minutes	**Per Serving** 321 calories, 22g fat (of which 8g saturates), 15g carbohydrate, 1.8g salt	Gluten free	**2**

Roasted Vegetable Salad with Mustard Mayonnaise

900g (2lb) mixed vegetables, such as fennel, courgettes, leeks, aubergines, baby turnips, new potatoes and red onions

2 garlic cloves, unpeeled

4–5 fresh marjoram or rosemary sprigs

5 tbsp olive oil

1 tsp flaked sea salt

mixed crushed peppercorns to taste

4 tsp balsamic vinegar

warm crusty bread to serve

For the mustard mayonnaise

150ml (¼ pint) mayonnaise

2 tbsp Dijon mustard

salt and ground black pepper

1 Preheat the oven to 220°C (200°C fan oven) mark 7. For the vegetables, quarter the fennel, chop the courgettes, leeks, aubergines and turnips and cut the onions into wedges. Place the vegetables, garlic, marjoram or rosemary, the oil, salt and peppercorns in a roasting tin and toss well (see Cook's Tip).

2 Cook in the oven for 30–35 minutes or until the vegetables are golden, tossing frequently. Sprinkle the vinegar over them and return to the oven for a further 5 minutes.

3 To make the mustard mayonnaise, mix together the mayonnaise and mustard, then season with salt and pepper and set aside.

4 Arrange the vegetable salad on a serving dish and serve with the mustard mayonnaise and crusty bread.

Cook's Tip

It's best to roast vegetables in a single layer or they will steam and become soggy. Use two tins if necessary.

Serves	EASY		NUTRITIONAL INFORMATION	
4	Preparation Time 15 minutes	Cooking Time 40 minutes	Per Serving 420 calories, 43g fat (of which 6g saturates), 5g carbohydrate, 1g salt	Gluten free Dairy free

Light Bites and Snacks

New Potato, Pea and Mint Frittatas

Goat's Cheese Parcels

Vegetable Tempura

Lemon Hummus with Black Olives

Cornbread

Roasted Vegetable and Rocket Tartlets

Poached Eggs with Mushrooms

Tomato Crostini with Feta and Basil

Sesame and Cabbage Rolls

Mini Poppadoms

Red Pepper Pesto Croûtes

New Potato, Pea and Mint Frittatas

3 tbsp olive oil, plus extra to grease

50g (2oz) Parmesan, grated

150g (5oz) baby new potatoes, roughly chopped

125g (4oz) freshly shelled peas – you'll need about 350g (12oz) peas in their pods

2 red onions, cut into thin wedges

1 tbsp freshly chopped mint

8 large eggs

142ml carton single cream

salt and ground black pepper

cherry tomato and leaf salad to serve

Freezing Tip

To freeze Complete the recipe, put the cooled frittatas in an airtight container and freeze. They will keep for up to one month.

To use Thaw overnight in the fridge, taking them out about 1 hour before you're ready to serve.

1 Preheat the oven to 180°C (160°C fan oven) mark 4. Lightly oil a deep 12-hole non-stick muffin tin. Sprinkle a pinch of Parmesan into each hole.

2 Cook the potatoes in lightly salted boiling water for about 5 minutes or until just tender. Add the peas to the potatoes for the last 3 minutes of cooking time. Drain well.

3 Heat the oil in a large, non-stick frying pan and fry the onions for 7–10 minutes until soft and golden. Add the drained vegetables and the mint. Cook, stirring, for 1 minute. Set aside to cool.

4 Beat the eggs in a large bowl with the cream and half the remaining Parmesan. Season well.

5 Divide the vegetables equally among the holes in the muffin tin, then pour in the egg mixture. Sprinkle with the remaining cheese. Cook for 20–25 minutes or until just set and golden. Cool in the tin for 20 minutes, then run a knife around the edge of each frittata and turn out on to a board. Leave to cool, then chill. The frittatas will keep for up to two days. Serve with the salad.

Serves	EASY		NUTRITIONAL INFORMATION	
6	**Preparation Time** 15 minutes, plus cooling	**Cooking Time** about 40 minutes	**Per Serving** 315 calories, 22.5g fat (of which 8g saturates), 12.6g carbohydrate, 0.6g salt	Gluten free

Cook's Tip

Be sure to keep the filo pastry covered with a damp cloth while making the pastries, to prevent it drying out and cracking.

Goat's Cheese Parcels

125g (4oz) fresh spinach leaves, blanched in boiling water for 1 minute and then drained

2 tbsp sunflower oil

1 onion, finely chopped

1 large garlic clove, chopped

250g (9oz) soft goat's cheese

270g pack filo pastry, thawed if frozen, cut into twenty-four 12.5cm (5in) squares (see Cook's Tip)

50g (2oz) butter, melted

sesame seeds to sprinkle

salt and ground black pepper

1 Run the drained, blanched spinach under very cold water. Once cold, squeeze out all the excess liquid and chop finely. Put to one side.

2 Heat the oil in a pan and add the onion and garlic. Cook until translucent, then allow to cool. Combine the spinach, onion mixture and goat's cheese in a bowl, and season generously.

3 Brush one square of filo with melted butter, cover with a second square and brush again. Put to one side and cover with a damp teatowel. Repeat with the remaining squares to make 12 sets. Put a dessertspoonful of filling in the centre of each square. Join up the corners to form a square parcel. Brush the pastry with a little more butter, sprinkle with sesame seeds and chill for 20 minutes. Meanwhile, preheat the oven to 220°C (200°C fan oven) mark 7.

4 Bake for 5 minutes or until the pastry is crisp and brown at the edges. Serve warm or cold.

Serves	A LITTLE EFFORT		NUTRITIONAL INFORMATION
6	**Preparation Time** 45 minutes, plus cooling and chilling	**Cooking Time** 10 minutes	**Per Serving** 345 calories, 22g fat (of which 12g saturates), 26g carbohydrate, 0.8g salt

125g (4oz) plain flour, plus 2 tbsp extra to sprinkle

2 tbsp cornflour

2 tbsp arrowroot

125g (4oz) cauliflower, cut into small florets

2 large carrots, peeled and cut into matchsticks

16 button mushrooms

2 courgettes, sliced

2 red peppers, seeded and sliced

vegetable oil for deep-frying

salt and ground black pepper

fresh coriander sprigs to garnish

For the dipping sauce

25g (1oz) fresh root ginger, peeled and grated

4 tbsp dry sherry

3 tbsp soy sauce

Vegetable Tempura

1 Sift the 125g (4oz) flour, the cornflour and arrowroot into a large bowl with a pinch each of salt and pepper. Gradually whisk in 300ml (½ pint) ice-cold water to form a thin batter. Cover and chill.

2 To make the dipping sauce, put the ginger, sherry and soy sauce in a heatproof bowl and pour in 200ml (7fl oz) boiling water. Stir well to mix, then set aside.

3 Put the vegetables in a large bowl and sprinkle with 2 tbsp flour. Toss well to coat. Heat the oil in a deep-fryer to 170°C (test by frying a small cube of bread; it should brown in 40 seconds). Alternatively, use a wok. Dip a handful of the vegetables in the batter, then remove with a slotted spoon, taking up a lot of the batter with the vegetables. Add to the hot oil and deep-fry for 3–5 minutes until crisp and golden. Remove with a slotted spoon and drain on kitchen paper; keep them hot while you cook the remaining batches. Serve immediately, garnished with coriander sprigs and accompanied by the dipping sauce.

A LITTLE EFFORT		NUTRITIONAL INFORMATION		Serves
Preparation Time 20 minutes	**Cooking Time** 15 minutes	**Per Serving** 450 calories, 21g fat (of which 3g saturates), 55g carbohydrate, 2.1g salt	Dairy free	**4**

Cook's Tip

Fresh garlic has juicy, mild cloves and is available from May and throughout the summer. It is the best garlic to use for making pesto, salsa verde, garlic mayonnaise and chilled soups.

Lemon Hummus with Black Olives

2 x 400g cans chickpeas, drained and rinsed

1 garlic clove (use fresh garlic when possible, see Cook's Tips), crushed

grated zest and juice of 1 lemon

4 tbsp olive oil

25g (1oz) pitted black olives, roughly chopped

1 tsp paprika, plus a little extra to serve

sticks of raw vegetables and breadsticks to serve

1 Put the chickpeas and garlic into a food processor. Add the lemon zest and juice and process to combine. With the motor running, drizzle in the oil to make a thick paste. If the hummus is too thick, add 1–2 tbsp cold water and blend again.

2 Spoon into a bowl and stir in the olives and paprika. Serve with a sprinkling of extra paprika with raw vegetables and breadsticks for dipping.

Serves 4	EASY		NUTRITIONAL INFORMATION	
	Preparation Time 15 minutes		**Per Serving** 284 calories, 16g fat (of which 2g saturates), 25g carbohydrate, 1.2g salt	Gluten free Dairy free

Cook's Tip

Serve warm with a bowl of soup for a substantial meal.

Cornbread

oil to grease

125g (4oz) plain flour

175g (6oz) polenta or cornmeal

1 tbsp baking powder

1 tbsp caster sugar

½ tsp salt

300ml (½ pint) buttermilk, or equal quantities of natural yogurt and milk, mixed together

2 medium eggs

4 tbsp extra virgin olive oil

butter to serve

1 Preheat the oven to 200°C (180°C fan oven) mark 6. Generously grease a shallow 20.5cm (8in) square tin.

2 Put the flour into a large bowl, then add the polenta or cornmeal, the baking powder, sugar and salt. Make a well in the centre and pour in the buttermilk or yogurt and milk mixture. Add the eggs and oil, then stir together until evenly mixed.

3 Pour into the tin and bake for 25–30 minutes until firm to the touch. Insert a skewer into the centre – if it comes out clean, the cornbread is done.

4 Leave the cornbread to rest in the tin for 5 minutes, then turn out and cut into chunky triangles. Serve warm with butter (see Cook's Tip).

EASY		NUTRITIONAL INFORMATION	Serves
Preparation Time 5 minutes	**Cooking Time** 25–30 minutes	**Per Serving** 229 calories, 8g fat (of which 1g saturates), 33g carbohydrate, 1.3g salt	**8**

Roasted Vegetable and Rocket Tartlets

375g pack ready-rolled puff pastry (preferably made with butter)

flour to dust

1 egg, beaten

2 tbsp coarse sea salt

300g (11oz) vegetable antipasti in oil (mixed roasted peppers, artichokes, onions, etc.)

a little olive oil (if needed)

2 tbsp balsamic vinegar

200g (7oz) red pepper hummus

50g (2oz) wild rocket

salt and ground black pepper

1 Preheat the oven to 220°C (200°C fan oven) mark 7. Unroll the puff pastry on a lightly floured surface and cut it into six equal-sized squares.

2 Lay the pastry squares on a large baking sheet and prick each one all over with a fork. Brush with the beaten egg and sprinkle the edges of each square with sea salt. Bake in the oven for 5–7 minutes until the pastry is golden brown and cooked through.

3 Pour off 4 tbsp oil from the antipasti (you may need to add a little extra oil) into a bowl. Add the vinegar, season well with salt and pepper, then set aside.

4 To serve, divide the hummus among the six pastry bases, spreading it over each one. Put each pastry square on an individual plate and spoon on the vegetable antipasti – there's no need to be neat. Whisk the reserved balsamic vinegar dressing together. Add the rocket leaves and toss to coat, then pile a small handful of leaves on top of each tartlet. Serve immediately.

EASY		NUTRITIONAL INFORMATION	Serves
Preparation Time 15 minutes	**Cooking Time** 5–7 minutes	**Per Serving** 378 calories, 28g fat (of which 1g saturates), 28g carbohydrate, 1.9g salt	**6**

Sesame and Cabbage Rolls

50g (2oz) dried shiitake mushrooms

3 tbsp sesame oil

4 garlic cloves, crushed

4 tbsp sesame seeds

450g (1lb) cabbage, finely shredded

1 bunch of spring onions, trimmed and chopped

225g can bamboo shoots, drained and rinsed

3 tbsp soy sauce

½ tsp caster sugar

2 x 270g packs filo pastry

1 large egg, beaten

vegetable oil for deep-frying

Spiced Plum Sauce or Thai Chilli Dipping Sauce to serve
(see Cook's Tips)

1 Put the mushrooms in a heatproof bowl and cover with boiling water. Soak for 20 minutes.

2 Heat the sesame oil in a wok or large frying pan. Add the garlic and sesame seeds and fry gently until golden brown. Add the cabbage and spring onions and fry, stirring, for 3 minutes. Drain and slice the mushrooms. Add them to the pan with the bamboo shoots, soy sauce and sugar and stir until well mixed. Remove the pan from the heat and leave to cool.

3 Cut the filo pastry into 24 x 18cm (7in) squares. Keep the filo squares covered with a damp teatowel as you work. Place one square of filo pastry on the worksurface and cover with a second square. Place a heaped tablespoonful of the cabbage mixture across the centre of the top square to within 2.5cm (1in) of the ends. Fold the 2.5cm (1in) ends of pastry over the filling. Brush one unfolded edge of the pastry with a little beaten egg, then roll up from the opposite edge to make a parcel. Shape the remaining pastry and filling in the same way to make 12 parcels.

4 Heat a 5cm (2in) depth of oil in a deep-fryer to 180°C (test by frying a small cube of bread; it should brown in 40 seconds). Alternatively, use a large, heavy-based saucepan. Fry the rolls in batches for about 3 minutes or until crisp and golden. Remove with a slotted spoon and drain on kitchen paper; keep them warm while you fry the remainder. Serve hot with a sauce for dipping (see Cook's Tips).

Cook's Tips

Spiced Plum Sauce: Slice 2 spring onions as thinly as possible. Put them in a small pan with 6 tbsp plum sauce, the juice of 1 lime, ½ tsp Chinese five-spice powder and 2 tbsp water. Heat gently for 2 minutes.

Thai Chilli Dipping Sauce: Put 200ml (7fl oz) white wine vinegar and 6 tbsp caster sugar in a small pan, bring to the boil and simmer for 2 minutes. Add 1 seeded and finely chopped red chilli (see page 35) and 50g (2oz) each finely chopped cucumber, onion and pineapple.

Makes 12	A LITTLE EFFORT		NUTRITIONAL INFORMATION	
	Preparation Time 30 minutes, plus soaking and cooling	**Cooking Time** about 15 minutes	**Per Roll** 224 calories, 13g fat (of which 2g saturates), 23g carbohydrate, 0.7g salt	Dairy free

Cook's Tip

Tahini is a thick, creamy paste that is made from ground sesame seeds. You can buy it in supermarkets and health food shops.

2 large aubergines

1–2 garlic cloves, crushed

1 tbsp tahini (see Cook's Tip)

juice of ½ lemon

3 tbsp freshly chopped coriander, plus extra sprigs to garnish

1 pack mini poppadoms (40 in pack)

salt and ground black pepper

paprika to garnish

Spicy Red Pepper Dip to serve (see page 19)

Mini Poppadoms

1 Preheat the oven to 200°C (180°C) mark 6. Pierce the aubergines several times with a sharp knife, put on a baking sheet and cook in the oven for about 1 hour or until very soft. Leave to cool.

2 Peel the aubergines. Wrap the flesh in a clean cloth and squeeze to remove any excess juice. Add the garlic, tahini and lemon juice and mash well with a fork or blend in a food processor. Stir in the chopped coriander and enough water to give a dipping consistency. Season with salt and pepper.

3 Put a little purée on each of the poppadoms and garnish with paprika and coriander sprigs.

Serves 8	EASY		NUTRITIONAL INFORMATION	
	Preparation Time 5 minutes, plus cooling	**Cooking Time** about 1 hour	**Per Serving** 128 calories, 6.2g fat (of which 1.1g saturates), 15.6g carbohydrate, 0.4g salt	Gluten free Dairy free

Red Pepper Pesto Croûtes

1 thin French stick, sliced into 24 rounds

olive oil to brush

ready-made pesto (see Cook's Tip)

4 pepper pieces (from a jar of marinated peppers), each sliced into 6 strips

pinenuts to garnish

1 Preheat the oven to 200°C (180°C fan oven) mark 6. Brush both sides of the bread with oil and put on a baking sheet. Cook in the oven for 15–20 minutes.

2 Spread 1 tsp pesto on each croûte, top with a pepper strip and pinenuts and serve.

Cook's Tip

- -

To make pesto, roughly chop 75g (3oz) basil, 50g (2oz) Parmesan, 25g (1oz) pinenuts and ½ crushed garlic clove and put in a food processor. With the motor running, add 50–75ml (2–3fl oz) extra virgin olive oil to make a paste. Season well with salt and pepper.

EASY		NUTRITIONAL INFORMATION	Serves
Preparation Time 20 minutes	**Cooking Time** 15–20 minutes	**Per Serving** 90 calories, 4.6g fat (of which 1g saturates), 9.6g carbohydrate, 0.3g salt	**24**

4

Easy Suppers

Couscous-stuffed Mushrooms

125g (4oz) couscous

20g pack fresh flat-leafed parsley, roughly chopped

280g jar mixed antipasti in oil, drained and oil
put to one side

8 large, flat large flat mushrooms

25g (1oz) butter

25g (1oz) plain flour

300ml (½ pint) skimmed milk

75g (3oz) mature Cheddar, grated, plus extra to sprinkle

green salad to serve

1 Preheat the oven to 220°C (200°C fan oven) mark 7. Put the couscous in a bowl with 200ml (7fl oz) boiling water, the parsley, antipasti and 1 tbsp of the reserved oil. Stir well.

2 Put the mushrooms on a non-stick baking tray and spoon a little of the couscous mixture into the centre of each. Cook in the oven while you make the sauce.

3 Meanwhile, whisk together the butter, flour and milk in a small pan over a high heat until the mixture comes to the boil. Reduce the heat as soon as it starts to thicken, then whisk constantly until smooth. Take the pan off the heat and stir in the cheese.

4 Spoon the sauce over the mushrooms and sprinkle with the remaining cheese. Put back into the oven for a further 7–10 minutes until golden. Serve with a green salad.

Serves	EASY		NUTRITIONAL INFORMATION
4	**Preparation Time** 3 minutes	**Cooking Time** about 12 minutes	**Per Serving** 340 calories, 21.1g fat (of which 8.9g saturates), 25.5g carbohydrate, 0.6g salt

Glamorgan Sausages

150g (5oz) Caerphilly cheese, grated
200g (7oz) fresh white breadcrumbs
3 spring onions, finely chopped
1 tbsp freshly chopped flat-leafed parsley
leaves from 4 thyme sprigs
3 large eggs, 1 separated
vegetable oil for frying
salt and ground black pepper
green salad and chutney to serve

1 Preheat the oven to 140°C (120°C fan oven) mark 1. Mix the cheese with 150g (5oz) breadcrumbs, the spring onions and herbs in a large bowl. Season well.

2 Add the 2 whole eggs plus the extra yolk and mix well to combine. Cover and chill for 5 minutes.

3 Lightly beat the egg white in a shallow bowl. Tip the rest of the breadcrumbs on to a large plate.

4 Take 2 tbsp of the cheese mixture and shape into a small sausage, about 4cm (1½in) long. Roll first in the egg white, then in the breadcrumbs to coat. Repeat to make 12 sausages in total.

5 Heat 2 tsp oil in a large heavy-based pan until hot and fry the sausages in two batches for 6–8 minutes, turning until golden all over. Keep warm in the oven while cooking the rest. Serve with salad and chutney.

Serves 4	EASY		NUTRITIONAL INFORMATION
	Preparation Time 25 minutes	**Cooking Time** 15 minutes	**Per Serving** 403 calories, 20.1g fat (of which 9.1g saturates), 39g carbohydrate, 1.7g salt

Cook's Tip

Piperade originates from the Basque region of France and traditionally contains lightly scrambled eggs mixed with onion, garlic, tomatoes and peppers.

2 tbsp olive oil

1 medium onion, finely chopped

1 garlic clove, finely chopped

1 red pepper, seeded and chopped

375g (13oz) tomatoes, peeled, seeded and chopped

pinch of cayenne pepper

8 large eggs

salt and ground black pepper

freshly chopped flat-leafed parsley to garnish

fresh bread to serve

Piperade

1 Heat the oil in a heavy-based frying pan. Add the onion and garlic and cook gently for 5 minutes. Add the red pepper and cook for 10 minutes or until softened.

2 Add the tomatoes, increase the heat and cook until they are reduced to a thick pulp. Season well with cayenne pepper, salt and pepper.

3 Lightly whisk the eggs and add to the frying pan. Using a wooden spoon, stir gently until they've just begun to set but are still creamy. Garnish with parsley and serve with bread.

EASY		NUTRITIONAL INFORMATION		Serves
Preparation Time 20 minutes	**Cooking Time** 20 minutes	**Per Serving** 232 calories, 17g fat (of which 4g saturates), 7g carbohydrate, 0.4g salt	Gluten free Dairy free	**4**

200g (7oz) firm tofu

4 tbsp sweet chilli sauce

2 tbsp light soy sauce

1 tbsp sesame seeds

2 tbsp toasted sesame oil

600g (1lb 5oz) ready-prepared mixed stir-fry vegetables, such as carrots, broccoli, mangetouts and bean sprouts

a handful of pea shoots or young salad leaves to garnish

rice to serve

Sweet Chilli Tofu Stir-fry

1 Drain the tofu, pat it dry and cut it into large cubes. Put the tofu in a shallow container and pour 1 tbsp sweet chilli sauce and 1 tbsp light soy sauce over it. Cover and marinate for 10 minutes.

2 Meanwhile, toast the sesame seeds in a hot wok or large frying pan until golden. Tip on to a plate.

3 Return the wok or frying pan to the heat and add 1 tbsp sesame oil. Add the marinated tofu and stir-fry for 5 minutes until golden. Remove and set aside.

4 Heat the remaining 1 tbsp oil in the pan, add the vegetables and stir-fry for 3–4 minutes until just tender. Stir in the cooked tofu.

5 Pour the remaining sweet chilli sauce and soy sauce into the pan, toss well and cook for a further minute until heated through. Sprinkle with the toasted sesame seeds and pea shoots or salad leaves, and serve immediately, with rice.

Serves 4	EASY		NUTRITIONAL INFORMATION	
	Preparation Time 5 minutes, plus 10 minutes marinating	**Cooking Time** 12 minutes	**Per Serving** 167 calories, 11g fat (of which 2g saturates), 5g carbohydrate, 1.6g salt	Dairy free

Egg and Pepper Pizza

150g (5oz) red and yellow marinated peppers in oil, drained and oil put to one side

8 tbsp passata

4 small wheat-free pizza bases

4 medium eggs

125g (4oz) watercress, washed and stalks removed

1 Preheat the oven to 220°C (200°C fan oven) mark 7 and preheat two large baking sheets, big enough to hold two pizzas each.

2 Chop the peppers into thin strips. Spoon 2 tbsp passata on to each pizza base and scatter strips of pepper around the edges. Make a dip in the passata in the middle of each pizza and break an egg into it. Carefully slide the pizzas on to the preheated baking sheets. Place in the oven and cook for 12 minutes until the eggs are thoroughly cooked.

3 Top the pizzas with the watercress, drizzle with a little of the reserved oil from the peppers and serve.

EASY		NUTRITIONAL INFORMATION		Serves
Preparation Time 15 minutes	**Cooking Time** 12 minutes	**Per Serving** 403 calories, 13g fat (of which 2g saturates), 61g carbohydrate, 1g salt	Gluten free Dairy free	**4**

Curried Tofu Burgers

1 tbsp sunflower oil, plus extra to fry

1 large carrot, peeled and finely grated

1 large onion, peeled and finely grated

2 tsp coriander seeds, finely crushed (optional)

1 garlic clove, crushed

1 tsp curry paste

1 tsp tomato purée

225g pack tofu

25g (1oz) fresh wholemeal breadcrumbs

25g (1oz) mixed nuts, finely chopped

plain flour to dust

salt and ground black pepper

rice and green vegetables to serve

1 Heat the oil in a large frying pan. Add the carrot and onion and fry for 3–4 minutes until the vegetables are softened, stirring all the time. Add the coriander seeds, if using, the garlic, curry paste and tomato purée. Increase the heat and cook for 2 minutes, stirring all the time.

2 Mash the tofu with a potato masher, then stir in the vegetables, breadcrumbs and nuts. Season with salt and pepper and beat thoroughly until the mixture starts to stick together. With floured hands, shape the mixture into eight burgers.

3 Heat some oil in a frying pan and fry the burgers for 3–4 minutes on each side until golden brown. Alternatively, brush lightly with oil and cook under a hot grill for about 3 minutes on each side or until golden brown. Drain on kitchen paper and serve hot, with rice and green vegetables.

EASY		NUTRITIONAL INFORMATION		Serves
Preparation Time 20 minutes	**Cooking Time** 6–8 minutes	**Per Serving** 253 calories, 18.4g fat (of which 2.7g saturates), 15.3g carbohydrate, 0.2g salt	Dairy free	**4**

Cook's Tip

Choose bags or bunches of fresh basil, as the larger leaves have a stronger, more peppery flavour than those of the plants sold in pots.

Aubergine Parmigiana

2 large aubergines, thinly sliced lengthways

2 tbsp olive oil, plus extra to brush

3 fat garlic cloves, sliced

2 x 200ml tubs fresh Napoletana sauce

4 ready-roasted red peppers, roughly chopped

20g (¾oz) fresh basil, roughly chopped (see Cook's Tip)

150g (5oz) Taleggio or fontina cheese, coarsely grated

50g (2oz) Parmesan, coarsely grated

salt and ground black pepper

green salad to serve

1 Preheat the oven to 200°C (180°C fan oven) mark 6, and preheat the grill until hot. Put the aubergines on an oiled baking sheet, brush with oil, scatter with the garlic and season with salt and pepper. Grill for 5–6 minutes until golden.

2 Spread a little Napoletana sauce over the bottom of an oiled ovenproof dish, then cover with a layer of aubergine and peppers, packing the layers together as tightly as you can. Sprinkle a little basil and some of each cheese over the top. Repeat the layers, finishing with a layer of cheese. Season with pepper. Cook in the oven for 20 minutes or until golden. Serve hot with a green salad.

Serves 4	EASY		NUTRITIONAL INFORMATION	
	Preparation Time 10 minutes	**Cooking Time** about 25 minutes	**Per Serving** 432 calories, 27.9g fat (of which 10.8g saturates), 24.8g carbohydrate, 2.4g salt	Gluten free

Cook's Tip

If you can't find pumpkin, use butternut squash.

50g (2oz) butter

175g (6oz) onion, finely chopped

900g (2lb) pumpkin, halved, peeled, seeded and cut into small cubes

2 garlic cloves, crushed

225g (8oz) Arborio (risotto) rice

600ml (1 pint) hot vegetable stock

grated zest of ½ orange

40g (1½oz) Parmesan, shaved

salt and ground black pepper

For the hazelnut butter

50g (2oz) hazelnuts

125g (4oz) butter, softened

2 tbsp freshly chopped flat-leafed parsley

Pumpkin Risotto with Hazelnut Butter

1 To make the hazelnut butter, spread the hazelnuts on a baking sheet and toast under a hot grill until golden brown, turning frequently. Put the nuts in a clean teatowel and rub off the skins, then chop finely. Put the nuts, butter and parsley on a piece of non-stick baking parchment. Season with pepper and mix together. Mould into a sausage shape, twist the baking parchment at both ends and chill.

2 To make the risotto, melt the butter in a large pan and fry the onion until soft but not coloured. Add the pumpkin and sauté over a low heat for 5–8 minutes until just beginning to soften. Add the garlic and rice and stir until well mixed. Increase the heat to medium and add the stock a little at a time, allowing the liquid to be absorbed after each addition. This will take about 25 minutes.

3 Stir in the orange zest and Parmesan and season with salt and pepper. Serve the risotto with a slice of the hazelnut butter melting on top.

EASY		NUTRITIONAL INFORMATION		Serves
Preparation Time 15 minutes	**Cooking Time** 40 minutes	**Per Serving** 706 calories, 50g fat (of which 27g saturates), 51g carbohydrate, 1.1g salt	Gluten free	**4**

Very Easy Four-cheese Gnocchi

350g pack fresh gnocchi

300g tub fresh four-cheese sauce

240g pack sunblush tomatoes

2 tbsp freshly torn basil leaves

1 tbsp freshly grated Parmesan

15g (½oz) butter, chopped

salt and ground black pepper

salad to serve

1 Bring a large pan of water to the boil, then add 1 tsp salt and the gnocchi and cook according to the packet instructions or until all the gnocchi have floated to the surface. Drain well and put the gnocchi back into the pan.

2 Preheat the grill. Add the four-cheese sauce and tomatoes to the gnocchi and heat gently, stirring, for 2 minutes.

3 Season with salt and pepper, then add the basil and stir again. Spoon into individual heatproof bowls, sprinkle a little Parmesan over each one and dot with butter.

4 Cook under the grill for 3–5 minutes until golden and bubbling. Serve with salad.

Serves 2	EASY		NUTRITIONAL INFORMATION	
	Preparation Time 3 minutes	Cooking Time 10 minutes	Per Serving 630 calories, 28g fat (of which 15g saturates), 77g carbohydrate, 00g salt	Gluten free

Try Something Different

Blend 25g (1oz) mild goat's cheese with 1 tbsp crème fraîche and put in the centre of the omelette before folding.

Classic French Omelette

2–3 medium eggs

1 tbsp milk or water

25g (1oz) unsalted butter

salt and ground black pepper

sliced or grilled tomatoes and freshly chopped flat-leafed parsley to serve

1 Whisk the eggs in a bowl, just enough to break them down – over-beating spoils the texture of the omelette. Season and add the milk or water.

2 Heat the butter in an 18cm (7in) omelette pan or non-stick frying pan until it is foaming, but not brown. Add the eggs and stir gently with a fork or wooden spatula, drawing the mixture from the sides to the centre as it sets and letting the liquid egg in the centre run to the sides. When set, stop stirring and cook for 30 seconds or until the omelette is golden brown underneath and still creamy on top; don't overcook.

3 Tilt the pan away from you slightly and use a palette knife to fold over one-third of the omelette to the centre, then fold over the opposite third. Slide the omelette out on to a warmed plate, letting it flip over so that the folded sides are underneath. Serve immediately, with tomatoes, sprinkled with parsley.

EASY		NUTRITIONAL INFORMATION		Serves
Preparation Time 5 minutes	**Cooking Time** 5 minutes	**Per Serving** 449 calories, 40g fat (of which 19g saturates), 1g carbohydrate, 1g salt	Gluten free	**1**

Papardelle with Spinach

350g (12oz) pappardelle

350g (12oz) baby leaf spinach, roughly chopped

2 tbsp olive oil

75g (3oz) ricotta

freshly grated nutmeg

salt and ground black pepper

1 Cook the pappardelle in a large pan of boiling water according to the packet instructions.

2 Drain the pasta well, return to the pan and add the spinach, oil and ricotta, tossing for 10–15 seconds or until the spinach has wilted. Season with a little nutmeg, salt and pepper and serve immediately.

Serves 4	EASY		NUTRITIONAL INFORMATION
	Preparation Time 5 minutes	**Cooking Time** 12 minutes	**Per Serving** 404 calories, 11g fat (of which 3g saturates), 67g carbohydrate, 0.3g salt

Cook's Tip

Tamari is a wheat-free Japanese soy sauce. It is available in large supermarkets and Asian food shops.

2 tbsp toasted sesame seeds

2 tbsp tamari (see Cook's Tip)

1 tsp light muscovado sugar

1 tsp rice wine vinegar

1 tbsp sesame oil

225g (8oz) smoked tofu, cubed

½ small white or green cabbage, shredded

2 carrots, peeled and cut into strips

200g (7oz) bean sprouts

4 roasted red peppers, roughly chopped

2 spring onions, shredded

brown rice to serve

Smoked Sesame Tofu

1 Put the sesame seeds into a bowl, add the tamari, sugar, vinegar and ½ tbsp sesame oil. Mix together, then add the smoked tofu and stir to coat. Set aside to marinate for 10 minutes.

2 Heat a large wok or non-stick frying pan, add the marinated tofu, reserving the marinade, and fry for 5 minutes until golden all over. Remove from the wok with a slotted spoon and set aside.

3 Heat the remaining oil in the wok, add the cabbage and carrots and stir-fry for 5 minutes. Stir in the bean sprouts, peppers, spring onions, cooked tofu and reserved marinade and cook for a further 2 minutes. Serve with brown rice.

EASY		NUTRITIONAL INFORMATION		Serves
Preparation Time 20 minutes, plus 10 minutes marinating	**Cooking Time** 12 minutes	**Per Serving** 208 calories, 11g fat (of which 2g saturates), 19g carbohydrate, 1.4g salt	Gluten free Dairy free	**4**

Chickpea Patties

2 x 400g cans chickpeas, drained and rinsed

4 garlic cloves, crushed

1 tsp ground cumin

1 small red onion, chopped

20g pack fresh coriander

2 tbsp plain flour, plus extra to dust

olive oil for frying

mixed salad and lemon wedges to serve

1 Pat the chickpeas dry with kitchen paper then put them into a food processor with the garlic, cumin, onion and coriander. Blend until smooth, then stir in the flour.

2 With floured hands, shape the chickpea mixture into 12 small, round patties and chill in the fridge for 20 minutes.

3 Heat a little oil in a non-stick frying pan over a medium heat and fry the patties in batches for about 2 minutes on each side or until heated through and golden. Serve warm with mixed salad and lemon wedges.

Freezing Tip

To freeze Make the patties, then cool, put in a freezerproof container and freeze. They will keep for up to one month.
To use Thaw overnight at a cool room temperature, then reheat in the oven at 180°C (160°C fan oven) mark 4 for 20 minutes.

Serves 4	EASY		NUTRITIONAL INFORMATION	
	Preparation Time 20 minutes, plus chilling	**Cooking Time** about 15 minutes	**Per Serving** 344 calories, 16.8g fat (of which 2.2g saturates), 36.6g carbohydrate, 1g salt	Dairy free

Try Something Different

Use a different cheese, such as Stilton.

Spinach and Goat's Cheese Frittata

200g (7oz) baby leeks, chopped

4 spring onions, chopped

125g (4oz) baby leaf spinach

6 large eggs

4 tbsp milk

freshly grated nutmeg

125g (4oz) soft goat's cheese, chopped

1 tbsp olive oil

salt and ground black pepper

mixed salad leaves to serve

1 Preheat the grill to high. Blanch the leeks in a pan of lighty salted boiling water for 2 minutes. Add the spring onions and spinach just before the end, of the cooking time. Drain, rinse in cold water and dry on kitchen paper.

2 In a bowl, whisk together the eggs, milk and nutmeg. Season with salt and pepper. Stir the goat's cheese into the egg mixture with the leeks, spinach and spring onions.

3 Heat the oil in a non-stick frying pan. Pour in the frittata mixture and fry gently for 4–5 minutes, then finish under the hot grill for 4–5 minutes until the top is golden and just firm. Serve with mixed salad leaves.

Serves 4	EASY		NUTRITIONAL INFORMATION	
	Preparation Time 10 minutes	Cooking Time 12 minutes	Per Serving 281 calories, 21.3g fat (of which 8.9g saturates), 3.3g carbohydrate, 0.9g salt	Gluten free

Pea, Mint and Ricotta Pasta

300g (11oz) farfalle pasta
200g (7oz) frozen peas
175g (6oz) ricotta
3 tbsp freshly chopped mint
2 tbsp extra virgin olive oil
salt and ground black pepper

1 Cook the pasta according to the packet instructions. Add the frozen peas for the last 4 minutes of cooking.

2 Drain the pasta and peas, reserving a ladleful of pasta cooking water, then return to the pan. Stir in the ricotta and mint with the pasta water. Season well, drizzle with the oil and serve at once.

EASY		NUTRITIONAL INFORMATION	Serves
Preparation Time 5 minutes	**Cooking Time** 10 minutes	**Per Serving** 431 calories, 14g fat (of which 5.1g saturates), 63.2g carbohydrate, 0g salt	**4**

Pasta with Vegetables, Pinenuts and Pesto

300g (11oz) penne pasta

50g (2oz) pinenuts

1 tbsp olive oil

1 garlic clove, crushed

250g (9oz) closed cup mushrooms, sliced

2 courgettes, sliced

250g (9oz) cherry tomatoes

6 tbsp fresh pesto

25g (1oz) Parmesan, shaved

1 Cook the pasta according to the packet instructions.

2 Meanwhile, gently toast the pinenuts in a dry frying pan, tossing them around until golden, then remove from the pan and set aside. Add the oil to the pan, then add the garlic, mushrooms and courgettes. Add a splash of water to the pan, then cover and cook for 4–5 minutes.

3 Uncover and add the tomatoes, then cook for a further 1–2 minutes. Drain the pasta and return to the pan. Add the vegetables, pinenuts and pesto to the drained pasta. Toss well to combine and serve immediately, topped with shaved Parmesan.

EASY		NUTRITIONAL INFORMATION	Serves
Preparation Time 5 minutes	**Cooking Time** 15 minutes	**Per Serving** 556 calories, 27.4g fat (of which 5.9g saturates), 59.5g carbohydrate, 0.5g salt	**4**

Cooking for Friends

Mushroom and Roasted Potato Bake

900g (2lb) small potatoes, peeled and quartered

6 tbsp olive oil

225g (8oz) onions, roughly chopped

450g (1lb) mixed mushrooms, such as shiitake and brown-cap, roughly chopped

2 garlic cloves, crushed

2 tbsp tomato purée

4 tbsp sun-dried tomato paste

25g (1oz) dried porcini mushrooms (optional)

2 tsp freshly chopped thyme

300ml (½ pint) dry white wine

300ml (½ pint) vegetable stock

284ml carton double cream

400g (14oz) large fresh spinach leaves, roughly chopped

175g (6oz) Gruyère cheese, grated

125g (4oz) Parmesan, grated

300g (11oz pint) Greek yogurt

2 medium eggs, beaten

salt and ground black pepper

fresh flat-leafed parsley and thyme sprigs to garnish (optional)

seasonal green vegetables to serve

1 Preheat the oven to 200°C (180°C fan oven) mark 6. Toss the potatoes with 4 tbsp oil in a large roasting tin and cook in the oven for 40 minutes or until tender and golden.

2 Meanwhile heat the remaining oil in a large, heavy-based pan. Add the onions and cook for 10 minutes or until soft, then add the chopped mixed mushrooms and garlic and cook over a high heat for 5 minutes. Stir in the tomato and purée paste, porcini mushrooms, if using, and the thyme and wine. Bring to the boil and simmer for 2 minutes.

3 Add the stock and cream, bring back to the boil and bubble for 20 minutes or until well reduced and syrupy. Pour into a 2.4 litre (4 pint) ovenproof dish. Stir in the potatoes, spinach, Gruyère and half the Parmesan. Season well with salt and pepper.

4 Combine the yogurt with the eggs and season. Spoon over the vegetable mixture and sprinkle with the remaining Parmesan.

5 Cook in the oven for 30–35 minutes until golden and bubbling. Garnish with parsley and thyme sprigs, if you like, and serve with green vegetables.

Serves 6	EASY		NUTRITIONAL INFORMATION
	Preparation Time 15 minutes	**Cooking Time** 1¼ hours	**Per Serving** 720 calories, 54g fat (of which 29g saturates), 30g carbohydrate, 1.7g salt

Freezing Tip

To freeze Complete the recipe to the end of step 3, cool, cover and freeze for up to one month.

To use Cook from frozen for 45 minutes, then unwrap the foil slightly and cook for a further 15 minutes until turning golden.

White Nut Roast

40g (1½oz) butter, plus extra to grease

1 onion, finely chopped

1 garlic clove, crushed

225g (8oz) mixed white nuts, such as brazils, macadamias, pinenuts and whole almonds, ground in a food processor

125g (4oz) fresh white breadcrumbs

grated zest and juice of ½ lemon

75g (3oz) sage Derby cheese or Parmesan, grated

125g (4oz) cooked, peeled (or vacuum-packed) chestnuts, roughly chopped

½ x 400g can artichoke hearts, drained and roughly chopped

1 medium egg, lightly beaten

2 tsp each freshly chopped parsley, sage and thyme, plus extra sprigs

salt and ground black pepper

tomato and red onion salad to serve

1 Preheat the oven to 200°C (180°C fan oven) mark 6. Melt the butter in a pan and cook the onion and garlic for 5 minutes or until soft. Put into a large bowl and set aside to cool.

2 Add the nuts, breadcrumbs, zest and juice of the lemon, cheese, chestnuts and artichokes to the onion and garlic. Season well and bind together with the egg. Stir in the chopped herbs.

3 Put the mixture on to a large piece of buttered foil and shape into a fat sausage, packing tightly. Scatter with the extra herb sprigs and wrap in the foil.

4 Cook on a baking sheet for 35 minutes, then unwrap the foil slightly and cook for a further 15 minutes until turning golden. Serve with salad.

Serves 8	EASY		NUTRITIONAL INFORMATION
	Preparation Time 20 minutes	**Cooking Time** about 1 hour	**Per Serving** 371 calories, 28g fat (of which 9g saturates), 20g carbohydrate, 0.8g salt

Cook's Tip

Yogurt Sauce: Mix together 225g (8oz) Greek yogurt, 1 crushed garlic clove and 2 tbsp freshly chopped coriander. Season with salt and pepper. Chill until ready to serve.

Spicy Vegetable Kebabs

12 baby onions

12 new potatoes, scrubbed

12 button mushrooms

2 courgettes

2 garlic cloves, crushed

1 tsp ground coriander

1 tsp turmeric

½ tsp ground cumin

1 tbsp sun-dried tomato paste

1 tsp chilli sauce

juice of ½ lemon

4 tbsp olive oil

275g (10oz) smoked tofu, cut into 2.5cm (1in) cubes

salt and ground black pepper

Yogurt Sauce (see Cook's Tip) and lemon wedges to serve

1 Blanch the onions in a pan of lightly salted boiling water for 3 minutes; drain, refresh in cold water and peel. Put the potatoes into a pan of cold salted water, bring to the boil and parboil for 8 minutes; drain and refresh under cold water. Blanch the mushrooms in boiling water for 1 minute; drain and refresh under cold water. Cut each courgette into six chunky slices and blanch for 1 minute; drain and refresh.

2 Mix the garlic with the spices, tomato paste, chilli sauce, lemon juice and oil in a shallow dish. Season with salt and pepper. Add the well-drained vegetables and tofu and toss to coat. Cover and chill for several hours or overnight.

3 Preheat the barbecue or grill. Soak six wooden skewers in water for 20 minutes. Thread the vegetables and tofu on to the skewers. Cook the kebabs for 8–10 minutes until the vegetables are charred and tender, turning frequently and basting with the marinade. Serve with Yogurt Sauce and lemon wedges.

EASY		NUTRITIONAL INFORMATION		Serves
Preparation Time 30 minutes, plus marinating	**Cooking Time** 25 minutes	**Per Serving** 247 calories, 14g fat (of which 3g saturates), 22g carbohydrate, 0.1g salt	Gluten free	**6**

Try Something Different

Use sliced sweet potatoes, or butternut squash, seeded and cut into chunks, instead of the potatoes.

Vegetable Moussaka

450g (1lb) potatoes, peeled and cut lengthways into 5mm (¼in) slices

1 aubergine, sliced into rounds

1 large red onion, peeled and cut into wedges

2 red peppers, seeded and sliced

4 tbsp olive oil

2 tbsp chopped thyme

225g (8oz) tomatoes, thickly sliced

2 garlic cloves, sliced

250g (9oz) passata

250g (9oz) soft goat's cheese

300g (11oz) natural yogurt

3 medium eggs

25g (1oz) Parmesan, grated

salt and ground black pepper

green salad to serve

1 Preheat the oven to 230°C (210°C fan oven) mark 8. Boil the potatoes in a pan of salted water for 5 minutes. Drain and put into a large roasting tin with the aubergine, onion and peppers. Drizzle with oil, add the thyme, toss and season with salt and pepper. Roast for 30 minutes, stirring occasionally.

2 Add the tomatoes and garlic and roast for 15 minutes, then take out of the oven. Reduce the oven temperature to 200°C (180°C fan oven) mark 6.

3 Put half the vegetables in a 1.7 litre (3 pint) ovenproof dish, then spoon half the passata over them and spread the goat's cheese on top. Repeat with the rest of the vegetables and passata. Mix together the yogurt, eggs and Parmesan. Season and then pour over the top. Cook in the oven for 45 minutes or until heated through. Serve with a green salad.

Serves	EASY		NUTRITIONAL INFORMATION	
6	**Preparation Time** 45 minutes	**Cooking Time** about 1½ hours	**Per Serving** 399 calories, 24g fat (of which 11g saturates), 29g carbohydrate, 1.2g salt	Gluten free

Cook's Tip

Oil-water spray is far lower in calories than oil alone and, as it sprays on thinly and evenly, you'll use less. Fill one-eighth of a travel-sized spray bottle with oil such as sunflower, light olive or vegetable (rapeseed) oil, then top up with water. To use, shake well before spraying. Store in the fridge.

Lentil Chilli

oil-water spray (see Cook's Tip)

2 red onions, chopped

1½ tsp each ground coriander and ground cumin

½ tsp ground paprika

2 garlic cloves, crushed

2 sun-dried tomatoes, chopped

¼ tsp crushed dried chilli flakes

125ml (4fl oz) red wine

300ml (½ pint) vegetable stock

2 x 400g cans brown or green lentils, drained and rinsed

2 x 400g cans chopped tomatoes

sugar to taste

salt and ground black pepper

natural low-fat yogurt and rice to serve

1 Spray a saucepan with the oil-water spray and cook the onions for 5 minutes until softened. Add the coriander, cumin and paprika. Combine the garlic, sun-dried tomatoes, chilli, wine and stock and add to the pan. Cover and simmer for 5–7 minutes. Uncover and simmer until the onions are very tender and the liquid has almost gone.

2 Stir in the lentils and tomatoes and season with salt and pepper. Simmer, uncovered, for 15 minutes until thick. Stir in sugar to taste. Remove from the heat.

3 Ladle out a quarter of the mixture and blend in a food processor or blender. Combine the puréed and unpuréed portions. Serve with yogurt and rice.

EASY		NUTRITIONAL INFORMATION		Serves
Preparation Time 10 minutes	**Cooking Time** 30 minutes	**Per Serving** 195 calories, 1.6g fat (of which 0.3 saturates), 32.4g carbohydrate, 0.1g salt	Gluten free Dairy free	**6**

Stuffed Aubergines

4 small aubergines

2 tbsp olive oil

25g (1oz) butter

1 small onion, very finely chopped

peeled 4 small ripe tomatoes, and roughly chopped

2 tsp chopped fresh basil or 1 tsp dried

2 medium eggs, hard-boiled and roughly chopped

1 tbsp capers

225g (8oz) fontina or Gruyère cheese, sliced

salt and ground black pepper

herby couscous to serve

1 Cut the aubergines in half lengthways and scoop out the flesh. Put the aubergine shells to one side.

2 Chop the aubergine flesh finely, then spread out on a plate and sprinkle with salt. Leave to stand for 20 minutes (this removes the bitter flavour), then turn into a colander. Rinse, drain and dry.

3 Heat half the oil in a frying pan with the butter or margarine, add the onion and fry gently for 5 minutes until soft but not coloured. Add the tomatoes, basil and salt and pepper to taste.

4 Meanwhile, put the aubergine shells in a single layer in an oiled ovenproof dish. Brush the insides with the remaining oil, then bake at 180°C (160°C fan oven) mark 4 for 10 minutes.

5 Spoon half the tomato mixture into the aubergine shells. Cover with a layer of egg, capers, then a layer of cheese. Spoon the remaining tomato mixture over the top. Bake for a further 15 minutes and serve sizzling hot with couscous.

Serves	EASY		NUTRITIONAL INFORMATION
4	**Preparation Time** 10 minutes, plus 20 minutes standing	**Cooking Time** 30 minutes	**Per Serving** 367 calories, 28.2g fat (of which 14.2g saturates), 7.7g carbohydrate, 1.7g salt

Tofu Laksa Curry

2 tbsp light soy sauce

½ red chilli, seeded and chopped (see page 35)

5cm (2in) piece of fresh root ginger, peeled and grated

250g pack fresh tofu

1 tbsp olive oil

1 onion, finely sliced

3 tbsp laksa paste

200ml (7fl oz) coconut milk

900ml (1½ pints) hot vegetable stock

200g (7oz) baby sweetcorn, halved lengthways

200g (7oz) fine green beans, trimmed

250g pack medium rice noodles

salt and ground black pepper

2 spring onions, sliced diagonally, 2 tbsp freshly chopped coriander and 1 lime, cut into four wedges, to garnish

1 Put the soy sauce, chilli and ginger in a bowl, add the tofu and leave to marinate for 30 minutes.

2 Heat the oil in a large pan. Add the onion and fry over a medium heat for 10 minutes, stirring, until golden. Add the laksa paste and cook for 2 minutes. Add the tofu, coconut milk, hot stock and sweetcorn and season with salt and pepper. Bring to the boil, add the green beans, reduce the heat and simmer for 8–10 minutes.

3 Meanwhile, put the noodles in a large bowl, pour boiling water over them and soak for 30 seconds. Drain, then stir into the curry. Pour into bowls and garnish with the spring onions, coriander and lime wedges. Serve immediately.

Serves 4	EASY		NUTRITIONAL INFORMATION	
	Preparation Time 15 minutes, plus 30 minutes marinating	**Cooking Time** 25 minutes	**Per Serving** 349 calories, 7.1g fat (of which 0.9g saturates), 63g carbohydrate, 2.7g salt	Dairy free

1 pumpkin, about 1.4–1.8kg (3–4lb)

2 tbsp olive oil

2 leeks, chopped

2 garlic cloves, crushed

2 tbsp freshly chopped thyme leaves

2 tsp paprika

1 tsp turmeric

125g (4oz) long-grain rice, cooked

2 tomatoes, peeled, seeded and diced

50g (2oz) cashew nuts, toasted and roughly chopped

125g (4oz) Cheddar, grated

salt and ground black pepper

Baked Stuffed Pumpkin

1 Cut a 5cm (2in) slice from the top of the pumpkin. Set aside for the lid. Scoop out and discard the seeds. Cut out most of the pumpkin flesh, leaving a thin shell. Cut the flesh into small pieces and set aside.

2 Heat the oil in a large pan, add the leeks, garlic, thyme, paprika and turmeric and fry for 10 minutes. Add the chopped pumpkin flesh and fry for a further 10 minutes until golden, stirring frequently to prevent sticking. Transfer the mixture to a large bowl. Preheat the oven to 180°C (160°C fan oven) mark 4.

3 Add the cooked rice to the pumpkin mixture along with the tomatoes, cashews and cheese. Fork through to mix and season with salt and pepper.

4 Spoon the stuffing mixture into the pumpkin shell, top with the lid and bake for 1¼–1½ hours until the pumpkin is softened and the skin is browned. Remove from the oven and leave to stand for 10 minutes. Cut into wedges to serve.

EASY		NUTRITIONAL INFORMATION		Serves
Preparation Time about 40 minutes	**Cooking Time** 1½ hours–1 hour 50 minutes, plus standing	**Per Serving** 438 calories, 24g fat (of which 9g saturates), 38g carbohydrate, 0.7g salt	Gluten free	**4**

275g (10oz) plain flour, plus extra to dust

1 tsp English mustard powder

175g (6oz) cold butter, cut into cubes

50g (2oz) mature Cheddar, grated

2 egg yolks, lightly beaten

900g (2lb) leeks, cut into 1cm (½in) slices, washed and drained

2 medium red onions, each cut into 8 wedges

juice of ½ lemon

leaves of 5 thyme sprigs

4 tbsp olive oil

1 small egg, lightly beaten

salt and ground black pepper

seasonal vegetables to serve

Easy Leek Pie

1 Put the flour, mustard powder, butter and ½ tsp salt into a food processor. Pulse until the mixture forms crumbs, then add the cheese, egg yolks and 2–3 tbsp cold water. Process briefly until the mixture comes together, then form into a ball, wrap in clingfilm and put in the freezer for 10 minutes.

2 Preheat the oven to 200°C (180°C fan oven) mark 6. Cook the leeks with 3 tbsp water in a covered pan until softened. Drain and set aside. Gently cook the onions and lemon juice in a covered pan until softened.

3 Roll out the pastry on a large, lightly floured sheet of baking parchment, to a 38cm (15in) round. Lift paper and pastry on to a baking sheet. Put the onions and leeks in the centre of the pastry, leaving a 7.5cm (3in) border. Sprinkle with the thyme, season with salt and pepper and drizzle with the oil. Fold the pastry edges over the filling. Brush the pastry rim with beaten egg. Bake for 50 minutes or until the vegetables are tender and serve with vegetables.

Serves	EASY		NUTRITIONAL INFORMATION
6	**Preparation Time** 15 minutes	**Cooking Time** 1 hour	**Per Serving** 571 calories, 39.4g fat (of which 19.5g saturates), 45.2g carbohydrate, 0.7g salt

Butternut Squash and Spinach Lasagne

1 butternut squash, peeled, halved, seeded and cut into 3cm (1¼in) cubes

2 tbsp olive oil

1 onion, sliced

25g (1oz) butter

25g (1oz) plain flour

600ml (1 pint) milk

250g (9oz) ricotta cheese

1 tsp freshly grated nutmeg

225g bag baby leaf spinach

6 'no need to pre-cook' lasagne sheets, about 100g (3½oz)

50g (2oz) pecorino cheese or Parmesan, grated

salt and ground black pepper

green salad to serve

1 Preheat the oven to 200°C (180°C fan oven) mark 6. Put the squash into a roasting tin with the oil, onion and 1 tbsp water. Mix well and season with salt and pepper. Roast for 25 minutes, tossing halfway through.

2 Melt the butter in a pan, stir in the flour and cook over a medium heat for 1–2 minutes. Gradually add the milk, stirring constantly. Simmer and cook, stirring, for 5 minutes or until the sauce has thickened. Break up the ricotta into the sauce and add the nutmeg. Mix together thoroughly and season to taste.

3 Heat 1 tbsp water in a pan. Add the spinach, cover and cook until the leaves are just wilted. Season generously. Spoon the squash and onion mixture into a 1.7 litre (3 pint) ovenproof dish. Layer the spinach on top, then cover with a third of the sauce, then the lasagne. Spoon the remaining sauce on top, season and sprinkle with the cheese. Bake for 30–35 minutes or until the topping is golden and the pasta cooked. Serve with green salad.

EASY		NUTRITIONAL INFORMATION	Serves
Preparation Time 30 minutes	**Cooking Time** about 1 hour	**Per Serving** 273 calories, 17g fat (of which 7.2g saturates), 17.5g carbohydrate, 0.6g salt	**6**

Wild Mushroom Pithiviers

450g (1lb) wild mushrooms

300ml (½ pint) milk

200ml (7fl oz) double cream

2 garlic cloves, crushed

450g (1lb) floury potatoes, thinly sliced

freshly grated nutmeg

50g (2oz) butter

2 tsp freshly chopped thyme, plus fresh sprigs to garnish

flour to dust

2 x 500g packs puff pastry, thawed if frozen

1 large egg, beaten

salt and ground black pepper

seasonal vegetables to serve

1 Rinse the mushrooms in cold running water to remove any grit, then pat dry with kitchen paper. Slice roughly.

2 Put the milk and cream in a large, heavy-based pan with the garlic. Bring to the boil, then add the potatoes. Bring back to the boil and simmer gently, stirring occasionally, for 15–20 minutes until the potatoes are tender. Season with salt, pepper and nutmeg. Leave to cool.

3 Meanwhile melt the butter in a large frying pan. When it's sizzling, add the mushrooms and cook over a high heat, stirring all the time, for 5–10 minutes until the mushrooms are cooked and the juices have evaporated completely. Season. Stir in the chopped thyme, then set aside to cool.

4 On a lightly floured surface, roll out the pastry thinly. Cut out eight rounds, approximately 12.5cm (5in) in diameter, for the tops and eight rounds, approximately 11.5cm (4½in) in diameter, for the bases. Put the smaller pastry rounds on baking sheets and brush the edges with beaten egg. Put a large spoonful of the cooled potato mixture in the centre of each round, leaving a 1cm (½in) border. Top with a spoonful of the mushroom mixture, then cover with the pastry tops. Press the edges together well to seal. Chill for 30 minutes–1 hour.

5 Preheat the oven to 220°C (200°C fan oven) mark 7 and put two baking trays in to heat up. Use the back of a knife to scallop the edges of the pastry and brush the top with the remaining beaten egg. If you like, use a knife to decorate the tops of the pithiviers.

6 Put the pithiviers, on their baking sheets, on the preheated baking trays. Cook for 15–20 minutes until a deep golden brown, swapping the trays around in the oven halfway through cooking. Garnish and serve with thyme sprigs with vegetables.

A LITTLE EFFORT		NUTRITIONAL INFORMATION	Serves
Preparation Time 1 hour, plus 1 hour chilling and cooling	**Cooking Time** about 1 hour	**Per Serving** 710 calories, 51g fat (of which 12g saturates), 58g carbohydrate, 1.2g salt	**8**

Caramelised Onion and Goat's Cheese Tart

230g ready-made uncooked shortcrust pastry case
275g jar onion confit
300g (11oz) mild soft goat's cheese, crumbled
1 medium egg, beaten
25g (1oz) Parmesan, grated
50g (2oz) wild rocket
balsamic vinegar and extra-virgin olive oil to drizzle
salt and ground black pepper

1 Preheat the oven to 200°C (180°C fan oven) mark 6. Line the pastry case with greaseproof paper, fill with baking beans and bake blind for 10 minutes. Remove the paper and beans, prick the pastry base all over with a fork and cook for a further 15–20 minutes until golden.

2 Spoon the onion confit into the pastry case. Beat the goat's cheese and egg together in a bowl until smooth, season with salt and pepper, then spoon on top of the onions. Level the surface with a knife and sprinkle with the Parmesan. Cook the tart for 25–30 minutes until the filling is set and just beginning to turn golden.

3 Leave to cool for 15 minutes, then cut away the sides of the foil case and carefully slide the tart on to a plate. Just before serving, arrange the rocket on top of the tart and drizzle with vinegar and oil. Serve warm.

Serves 6	EASY		NUTRITIONAL INFORMATION
	Preparation Time 10 minutes	**Cooking Time** 1 hour, plus 15 minutes cooling	**Per Serving** 480 calories, 28g fat (of which 14g saturates), 44g carbohydrate, 1.5g salt

Pasta Shells Stuffed with Spinach and Ricotta

450g (1lb) fresh spinach, washed

125g (4oz) ricotta

1 medium egg

pinch of freshly grated nutmeg

grated zest of ½ lemon

50g (2oz) freshly grated Parmesan

225g (8oz) conchiglione pasta shells

½ quantity of Classic Tomato Sauce (see page 18)

25g (1oz) pinenuts

salt and ground black pepper

1 Put the washed spinach in a large pan. Cover and cook over a low to medium heat for 2–3 minutes until wilted. Drain and squeeze out the excess liquid. Chop finely.

2 Put the spinach into a large bowl with the ricotta and beat in the egg. Stir in the grated nutmeg, lemon zest and 25g (1oz) grated Parmesan. Season.

3 Preheat the oven to 200°C (180°C fan oven) mark 6. Meanwhile, cook the pasta according to the packet instructions for oven-baked dishes. Drain well.

4 Spread the Classic Tomato Sauce in the bottom of an 18 x 23cm (7 x 9in) ovenproof dish. Fill the shells with spinach mixture and arrange on top of the sauce. Sprinkle with 25g (1oz) grated Parmesan and the pinenuts. Cook in the oven for 20–25 minutes until golden.

EASY		NUTRITIONAL INFORMATION	Serves
Preparation Time 10 minutes	**Cooking Time** about 45 minutes	**Per Serving** 430 calories, 17.3g fat (of which 6.5g saturates), 49.9g carbohydrate, 1.6g salt	**4**

Cook's Tip

This recipe uses sheets of lasagne wrapped around a filling to make cannelloni, but you can also buy dried cannelloni tubes, which can be filled using a teaspoon or a large icing bag fitted with a plain nozzle.

Mixed Mushroom Cannelloni

6 sheets fresh lasagne (see Cook's Tip)

3 tbsp olive oil

1 small onion, finely sliced

3 garlic cloves, sliced, a few slices kept to one side

20g pack fresh thyme, finely chopped, a little reserved for sprinkling

225g (8oz) chestnut or brown-cap mushrooms, 00roughly chopped

125g (4oz) flat-cap mushrooms, roughly chopped

2 x 125g goat's cheese logs, with rind

350g carton cheese sauce

salt and ground black pepper

mixed salad to serve

1 Preheat the oven to 180°C (160°C fan oven) mark 4. Cook the lasagne until just tender. Drain and rinse. Keep covered with cold water until ready to use.

2 Heat the oil in a pan. Add the onion and cook over a medium heat for 7–10 minutes until soft. Add the garlic and fry for 1–2 minutes. Add the thyme and mushrooms and cook for 5 minutes or until there is no excess liquid in the pan. Season, remove from the heat and set aside. Crumble one goat's cheese log into the cooled mushroom mixture and stir in.

3 Drain the lasagne and pat dry. Spoon 2–3 tbsp of the mushroom mixture along the long edge of each lasagne sheet, leaving a 1cm (½in) border. Roll up the pasta. Cut each roll in half. Put into a shallow ovenproof dish and spoon the cheese sauce over. Slice the remaining goat's cheese thickly. Arrange across the middle of the pasta. Sprinkle the reserved garlic and thyme on top. Cook in the oven for 30–35 minutes until bubbling. Serve with salad.

Serves 4	EASY		NUTRITIONAL INFORMATION
	Preparation Time 15 minutes	**Cooking Time** 46–55 minutes	**Per Serving** 623 calories, 37g fat (of which 18g saturates), 47g carbohydrate, 1.9g salt

Index

Collect the Easy To Makes!...

Good Housekeeping — Slow Cook — easy to make!

Good Housekeeping — Speedy Meals — easy to make!

Good Housekeeping — Chocolate — easy to make!

Good Housekeeping — Chicken — easy to make!

Good Housekeeping — Low GI — easy to make!

Good Housekeeping — Healthy Meals in Minutes — easy to make!

Good Housekeeping — Pies, Pies, Pies — easy to make!

Good Housekeeping — Cakes & Bakes — easy to make!

Good Housekeeping — Soups — easy to make!

Good Housekeeping — Family Meals in minutes — easy to make!

Good Housekeeping — Wok & Stir-fry — easy to make!

Good Housekeeping — One Pot — easy to make!

Good Housekeeping — Puddings & Desserts — easy to make!

Good Housekeeping — Roasts — easy to make!

Good Housekeeping — Salads & Dressings — easy to make!

Good Housekeeping — Everyday Family Meals — easy to make!

Good Housekeeping — Meat Free — easy to make!

Good Housekeeping — Cupcakes, Muffins and Brownies — easy to make!

Good Housekeeping — BBQ & Grills — easy to make!

Good Housekeeping — Christmas — easy to make!